# The Effects of the Republican Budgets Versus the President's Budget

*"Helping hardworking families make ends meet. Giving them the tools they need to get ahead in this new economy. Revving the engines of growth and competitiveness. That's what middle-class economics offers. This is where I believe America needs to go. And if we make these investments – in ourselves, in our prosperity, and in our future – then the economy won't just be stronger a year from now, or five years from now, it will be stronger for decades to come."*

*– President Obama, Remarks to the City Club of Cleveland, March 18, 2015*

## Executive Summary

With more than 12 million private-sector jobs created over the last 60 months, it is clear that the President's middle class economic agenda is working. But instead of taking the steps we need to strengthen the standing of working families, the Republican budgets for fiscal year (FY) 2016 would return our economy to the same top-down economics that has failed us before: cutting taxes for millionaires and billionaires, while slashing investments in the middle class that we need to grow the economy, like education, job training, and manufacturing. The Republican proposals stand in stark contrast to the President's FY 2016 Budget, which would bring middle class economics into the 21st Century.

The President's Budget builds on the progress we've made and shows what we can do if we invest in America's future and commit to an economy that rewards hard work, generates rising incomes, and allows everyone to share in the prosperity of a growing America. It lays out a strategy to strengthen our middle class and help America's hard-working families get ahead in a time of relentless economic and technological change. And it makes the critical investments needed to accelerate and sustain economic growth in the long run, including in research, education, training, and infrastructure.

Republicans have chosen different priorities. Yet again, they are seeking to balance the budget on the backs of the middle class and those struggling to get into the middle class, while cutting taxes for the wealthy and well-connected. They still won't say where many of their spending cuts come from. But they are clear that their budget would continue the harmful cuts known as sequestration in 2016, threatening economic growth, cutting programs that the middle-class, seniors, and children count on, and attempting to fund national security through irresponsible budget gimmicks. Their budgets slash domestic investments even more significantly after 2016, along with programs that serve the most vulnerable Americans. They also target health care. House Republicans have proposed to end Medicare as we know it, transforming it from a guarantee seniors can count on into a voucher program. And, despite the more than 16 million

1

Americans who have health insurance today after five years of the Affordable Care Act (ACA), both House and Senate Republicans are yet again proposing to repeal the law's coverage expansions. The Congressional Budget Office (CBO) estimates that the revenue and spending levels specified in the Republican budget would reduce the size of the economy over the next few years by about 0.5 percent, which could translate into more than a million lost job-years.

Meanwhile, in the same week they are voting on their budget resolution, House Republicans are also voting to repeal the estate tax, at a cost of hundreds of billions of dollars. Not only would estate tax repeal give away revenue their own budget counts on to balance, but the juxtaposition also shows where their priorities lie: cutting taxes for wealthy estates – the wealthiest 0.1 percent of Americans – while maintaining sequestration funding cuts that will deprive struggling families of access to Head Start, job training, and Housing Choice Vouchers that help provide affordable housing.

The choice could not be more clear or the consequences more stark. Thanks to President Obama and the resilience of the American people, the economy is growing again and creating jobs at the fastest pace since the 1990s. The Republican budgets would put that growth at risk and limit opportunity for the middle-class and those striving to join it.

**While claiming to prioritize fiscal responsibility, the Republican budgets would not ask the wealthy to contribute a single dollar to deficit reduction. The House budget even promises large new tax cuts for the wealthy and big corporations.** Among the few specific tax proposals in the House Republican budget is a promise to spend hundreds of billions on high-income and business tax cuts, with up to trillions more in unspecified high-income and corporate rate reductions. The proposals specified in the House Republican budget would cut taxes for millionaires by an average of more than $50,000, before even adding the proposed cuts to tax rates. Meanwhile, the Republican budgets do nothing to prevent a tax increase on 26 million working families and students. In the past, Congressional Republicans have made clear they would let this tax increase happen, raising taxes by an average of $900 apiece for 16 million working families (see state-by-state estimates in the appendix) and by $1,100 for 12 million families and students paying for college.

**Because Congressional Republicans refuse to ask millionaires and billionaires to pay their fair share or to raise a single dollar of new revenue, their budgets rely on the same, failed top-down economics as in previous years. Specifically, they would:**

- **Take away health insurance from more than 16 million people who have gained coverage after five years of the Affordable Care Act.** The Affordable Care Act is working. Thanks to its coverage provisions, the share of Americans without health insurance is at a historic low – and these provisions are costing almost one third less than the Congressional Budget Office (CBO) initially projected. Almost exactly five years after the ACA was enacted into law, Republicans will be voting for the more than 50th time to repeal these provisions. That would:

- Take away Marketplace coverage from 11.7 million Americans who have newly signed up or been re-enrolled in coverage for 2015 (see state-by-state estimates in the appendix). Some of these individuals would become uninsured, while others would end up with worse or less affordable coverage.
- Deprive up to 130 million Americans with pre-existing conditions of the security of knowing they will still be able to buy affordable health coverage if they lose their jobs or otherwise lose their health insurance;
- Deny millions of young adults up to age 26 the option to stay on their parents' plans if they re-enroll in school or get a job without health coverage; and
- Increase prescription drug costs for more than 5 million seniors and people with disabilities. (See state-by-state estimates in the appendix.)

- **Cut investments in the middle class by maintaining sequestration funding levels.** Under the Republican budgets, both non-defense and base defense discretionary funding in 2016 would be at the lowest real levels in a decade. Investments in the middle class would be heavily impacted: real preK-12 per pupil education funding would fall to its lowest levels since 2000, and real R&D funding would fall to its lowest level since 2002, except when large sequestration cuts also took effect in 2013. Compared to the President's Budget, the Republican budgets would result in:

  - 35,000 fewer children in Head Start.
  - $1.2 billion less in Title I education funding, enough to fund about 4,500 schools, 17,000 teachers and aides, and 1.9 million students.
  - $347 million less in IDEA funding, an amount that could support up to 6,000 special education teachers, paraprofessionals, and other related staff.
  - More than 2 million fewer workers receiving job training and employment services.
  - 1,300 fewer medical research grants at NIH.
  - 950 fewer competitive science research awards at the NSF, affecting 11,600 researchers, technicians and students.
  - Elimination of the Manufacturing Extension Partnerships, which serve 30,000 small manufacturers.
  - $2.1 billion less funding for Housing Choice Vouchers, resulting in 133,000 fewer families getting help. (See state-by-state estimates in the appendix.)
  - Prevention or delay of construction or renovation projects at over 125 national parks, including Denali, the Grand Canyon, and Yellowstone.

*(See state-by-state estimates for many of these impacts in the appendix.)*

Meanwhile, as a wide range of national security experts ranging from former Secretary of Defense Robert Gates to Ambassador John Bolton have pointed out, locking in sequestration for defense would undermine our readiness and efforts to secure technological superiority for U.S. forces in future conflicts. Instead of providing a plan to reverse sequestration, Congressional Republicans try to mask the fact that they do not responsibly fund our national security. The Republican budgets try to have it both ways on defense funding – maintaining sequestration and then using overseas contingency operations funds intended for wars and not subject to budget caps to fund the day-to-day operations of the Pentagon. As the Secretary of Defense and the Chairman of the Joint Chiefs have explained, this is both bad budgeting and harmful to military planning. Former House Budget Chairman Paul Ryan referred to it as treating overseas contingency funding as a "slush fund," and Senators Mike Crapo and Jeff Flake just last week called it a "gimmick."

- **Increase cuts to middle class investments starting in 2017.** Both the House and Senate Republican budgets cut these investments even more deeply after 2016. The House Budget in particular doubles, then triples its cuts relative to the President's Budget. If non-defense discretionary funding were cut 12 percent below sequestration levels in 2016 – the cut the Republican budget would make in 2018 – it would mean the following compared to the President's Budget:

    o More than 157,000 children would lose out on access to Head Start services.
    o Title I education funding would be $2.7 billion lower, enough to fund about 10,000 schools, 38,000 teachers, and aides, and 4.2 million students.
    o IDEA funding would be nearly $1.6 billion lower, an amount that could support up to 26,800 special education teachers, paraprofessionals, and other related staff.
    o More than 4 million workers would lose out on job training and employment services.

- **Reach their fiscal targets through unspecified cuts and gimmicks, plus deep cuts to programs that serve the most vulnerable.** On top of their cuts to middle-class investments and the ACA, the Republican budgets call for an additional nearly $2 trillion in cuts to health, safety net, and other mandatory programs. Their budgets (for the fifth year in a row in the case of the House) decline to specify where almost $1 trillion of these savings would come from. But they do single out a few programs as among the first places they would look to reduce the deficit:

    o **Pell Grants:** The Republican budgets eliminate mandatory funding for Pell Grants, and the House budget specifies that it would freeze the maximum grant at its current level, instead of allowing it to increase to keep pace with inflation. Over time, this would reduce financial aid for almost all of the more than 8 million students who rely on Pell Grants to afford college.
    o **Medicaid:** The budgets block grant Medicaid, cutting resources for Medicaid and the Children's Health Insurance Program (CHIP) by more than $900 billion in the case of the House, on top of the impact of repealing the ACA coverage provisions. Medicaid currently insures almost 70 million Americans in a typical month, including millions of children, seniors, and people with disabilities. The combination of repealing the ACA and the House Republican budget's Medicaid cuts would more than double the number of uninsured Americans.
    o **SNAP:** The House budget would convert the Supplemental Nutrition Assistance Program (SNAP) to a block grant, cutting funding by about $125 billion over the 2021-

2025 period and jeopardizing nutrition assistance for the more than 46 million Americans who depend on it, the majority of whom are children, seniors, and people with disabilities. Research has shown that SNAP not only helps families put food on the table, but also has a positive long-term impact on children's health and education outcomes. (While less specific, the SNAP cuts in the Senate budget appear to be at least as large.)

*(See state-by-state estimates for these impacts in the appendix.)*

Since even these cuts leave the Republican budgets short of their fiscal goals, they get the rest of the way there through:

- **Declining to implement their own policies in their budget.** While claiming to "repeal Obamacare" and stripping away health coverage from millions, the Republican budgets retain the ACA's savings, claiming they will replace the revenues through unspecified tax reforms. And while House Republicans have voted to extend hundreds of billions in business tax cuts without offsets, their budget adds up only by assuming those measures would be paid for.

- **Counting about $150 billion in deficit reduction from highly uncertain "dynamic scoring."** Not only is dynamic scoring uncertain in general, but the dynamic estimates of the Republican budgets take into account only their deficit reduction, not the long-term economic costs of their cuts to research, education, and other investments.

- **Terminating the FDIC's Orderly Liquidation Authority.** This authority was enacted to ensure taxpayer funds are never again used to bail out 'too big to fail' financial institutions. And though the House budget says it does "not rely on gimmicks or creative accounting tricks," the 'savings' from this termination are both, because, by law, any costs of the program must be recouped from the financial industry.

**The Republican budgets also propose other policy changes that would have severe consequences for seniors and the middle class.**

- **The House budget would end Medicare as we know it.** For new beneficiaries starting in 2024, the House Republican budgets would end Medicare as we know it by replacing guaranteed access to the traditional Medicare program with a voucher program, increasing costs for millions of seniors and forcing millions out of traditional Medicare, risking a death spiral as private plans siphon off healthier and less expensive beneficiaries. Beneficiaries would receive a premium-support payment that may not completely offset the premium for the Medicare plan of their choice (either a private plan or the traditional Medicare program). As CBO and numerous outside analysts have found, under a voucher system healthier, lower-cost Medicare beneficiaries would be more likely to enroll in private plans. Meanwhile, traditional Medicare would increasingly be left with sicker, more expensive beneficiaries.

- **Undercut important consumer protections.** In addition to cutting services and aid for the most vulnerable, the House Republican budget calls for rolling back key aspects of Wall Street Reform, while underfunding the agencies working to implement it. It terminates mandatory funding for the Consumer Financial Protection Bureau (CFPB), greatly limiting the independence of this watchdog for the rights of consumers. In addition, it risks returning us to the days of "too big to fail," protecting Wall Street firms from important regulatory safeguards and putting ordinary citizens and the economy at risk.

- **Do nothing to address our Nation's crumbling infrastructure.** The President has put forth a detailed plan to make significant investments in repairing and modernizing our surface transportation infrastructure, paid for as part of a pro-growth business tax reform that would close loopholes that let U.S. companies shift profits and jobs to tax havens. Not only do the Republican budgets lack a real plan to address the looming expiration and insolvency of the Highway Trust Fund (instead establishing only an unspecified reserve fund to "provide for innovative thinking"), but their sequestration cuts put funding for successful infrastructure programs like TIGER grants at risk.

Instead of the same top-down economics that led to the financial crisis, the President's Budget invests in an economy that puts the middle class first and cuts the deficit in a balanced way, including by closing tax loopholes to ensure that millionaires and billionaires pay their fair share. Now is the time to strengthen the standing of working and middle class families, not go back to the same failed top-down economics.

## I. The President's Plan for Fiscally Responsible Investment in Growth and Opportunity Versus Republican Proposals that would Harm the Economy, the Middle-Class, and the Most Vulnerable

The 2013 sequester was a costly, self-inflicted wound to our economy and middle-class families. The Congressional Budget Office estimated that the 2013 sequester cost the economy 750,000 jobs. Meanwhile, the sequester cut deep into all aspects of the discretionary budget, including research, education, and help for the most vulnerable. The National Institutes of Health (NIH) awarded 640 fewer competitive grants, resulting in the lowest number of new competitive grants in over a decade, and many more grantees were forced to narrow the scope or slow the pace of their research. More than 57,000 children lost access to Head Start, leading to the lowest enrollment since 2001, and nearly 20,000 fewer college students received work study jobs. The Department of Defense endured deep cuts to readiness, weathered civilian pay freezes and furloughs, and cut badly needed investments in modernization and critical technologies.

In 2014, policymakers on a bipartisan basis moved away from manufactured crises and austerity, helping to lay the groundwork for stronger growth and job market gains. The Bipartisan Budget Act of 2013, an agreement spearheaded by Senator Patty Murray and Representative Paul Ryan (the "Murray-Ryan agreement"), reversed a portion of sequestration and allowed for higher investment levels in 2014 and 2015. While it did not go far enough, the Murray-Ryan agreement contributed to an improving job market and accelerating growth and made room for important investments in domestic priorities ranging from early education to manufacturing, while also providing needed funds for national security.

A return to full sequestration in 2016 would bring discretionary funding to its lowest level, adjusted for inflation, since 2006. This is despite the fact that, since 2006, the U.S. population has grown by 7 percent, and costs in some key areas have grown much faster than inflation; for example, VA medical care costs have nearly doubled. Returning to 2006 funding levels would weaken America's security and weaken the economy at a time of accelerating growth.

### The President's Plan

The President's FY 2016 Budget builds on our economic progress by making needed investments that accelerate economic growth, and ensuring that all Americans have the opportunity to share in that growth. We cannot afford a return to mindless austerity, so the President's Budget ends sequestration[1], fully reversing it for domestic priorities in 2016, matched by equal dollar increases for defense. These investments are more than paid for with smart spending cuts, program integrity measures, and commonsense loophole closers.

---

[1] In this report, sequestration primarily refers to the discretionary cap reductions required by the failure of the Joint Select Committee on Deficit Reduction to propose, and the Congress to enact, legislation to reduce the deficit by $1.2 trillion over the FY 2013 through FY 2021 period.

The Budget helps middle-class families get ahead, with a package of tax cuts and targeted investments in child care, early education, and paid leave. The Budget invests in helping workers gain the skills they need for the new economy, through job training, apprenticeships, and the President's proposal to make two years of community college free for responsible students. It also ensures that the Pell Grant program remains a strong source of support for low- and moderate-income students by indexing grants to inflation, and it expands and simplifies education tax credits. The Budget builds a 21$^{st}$ century economy, with investments in manufacturing, infrastructure, and research and development. And it makes responsible investments in defense to protect our national security, allowing for the restoration of readiness and investment in modernization needed to ensure America's continued technological edge.

The President's Budget demonstrates that we do not have to choose between fiscal responsibility and investing in growth and opportunity. It achieves $1.8 trillion in deficit reduction over 10 years, primarily through reforms to health programs, the tax system, and our broken immigration system and without harming core safety net programs that support the most vulnerable. Overall, the President's proposals reduce deficits to below 3 percent of GDP, stabilize debt as a share of the economy, and put it on a declining path.

## The Congressional Republican Approach

### Locking in Sequestration for Domestic Investments and National Security

The Republican budgets maintain sequestration funding levels for both base defense and non-defense discretionary programs in 2016. Because the Republican budget resolutions do not provide specific discretionary program levels, this analysis assumes that required cuts would be distributed across-the-board relative to 2015 enacted funding levels. The resulting levels are then compared to those proposed in the President's FY 2016 Budget. [2] If Republicans chose to fund some programs above the levels assumed here, they would have to cut the remaining programs even more deeply.

**Education and Training**

Our future competitiveness and prosperity depend on the skills of our workforce. The Republican budgets would jeopardize funding for education and training at every level: from Head Start to K-12 education to programs that train and retrain adults for the jobs of the future.

**Early childhood.** Research demonstrates that supporting development when children are very young can produce large benefits to children, parents, and society. Early learning initiatives narrow the achievement gap, boost children's earnings later in life, and provide benefits that outweigh the costs, roughly $8.60 in benefits for every $1 spent. This includes Head Start, which

---

[2] More specifically, unavoidable cost growth in certain areas, such as veterans' medical care, means that sequestration funding levels for 2016 would require a 1.5 percent cut to non-defense discretionary relative to 2015.

research has shown has a direct impact on longer-term outcomes, including educational attainment and earnings.[3]

But when sequestration took effect in 2013, more than 57,000 children lost access to Head Start, leading to the lowest enrollment since 2001 (see Figure 1) and a permanently missed opportunity for these children. In an effort to prevent the loss of slots, programs around the country also cut 30,000 home visits, eliminated over 1.3 million days of service, and shortened school days by a total of 18,000 hours. New research finds that full-day full-year Head Start programs have larger impacts on learning, suggesting that sequestration cuts likely compromised Head Start quality for an even larger number of children than lost access to the program altogether.[4]

Motivated by the strong evidence that quality early childhood education improves long-term outcomes, the President's Budget provides a $1.5 billion increase for Head Start, both to ensure that all programs can provide full-day, full-year care and to ensure that the number of children served can return to 2014 levels. Compared to the President's Budget, the Republican budgets' funding levels would not only fail to provide the resources needed to support a more robust school day and school year, but would also lead more than 35,000 of the Nation's most vulnerable children to lose access to Head Start services.[5] *(See state-by-state estimates in the appendix.)*

**K-12 education.** A return to sequestration funding levels would also have severe consequences for key K-12 educational investments, with per-pupil education funding falling to the lowest level since 2000. Compared to the President's Budget, the 2016 funding levels put forward in the Republican budgets would mean:

- A $1.2 billion reduction in Title I, approximately equivalent to funding for nearly 4,500 schools, 17,000 teachers and aides, and 1.9 million students. *(See state-by-state estimates in the appendix.)* Furthermore, provisions in the House Republican Elementary and Secondary Education Act could hurt the most disadvantaged schools and districts even more by allowing states to send more money to wealthier districts.

---

[3] For additional discussion see "The Economics of Early Childhood Investments," published by the President's Council of Economic Advisors in December 2014 and updated in January 2015: https://www.whitehouse.gov/sites/default/files/docs/early_childhood_report1.pdf.

[4] "Inputs in the production of early childhood human capital: Evidence from Head Start." Walters, C., 2014 Working Paper: http://eml.berkeley.edu/~crwalters/papers/HS_2_2014.pdf.

[5] For Figure 1, for all years except FY 2015, PB 2016, and FY 2016 Sequester, source is Head Start statistics (found at https://eclkc.ohs.acf.hhs.gov/hslc/data/factsheets/2013-hs-program-factsheet.html). The term "funded enrollment" refers to the number of children and pregnant women that are supported by funds at any one time in the program year; these are usually referred to as slots. FY 2015 and PB 2016 funded enrollment levels are estimates, and can be found in the 2016 President's Budget Justification to Congress. FY 2016 Sequester enrollment levels are also estimates. These estimates do not include Early Head Start-Child Care Partnership slots. Estimates use a blended cost per slot across Head Start and Early Head Start.

- A $347 million reduction in IDEA, an amount equivalent to what is necessary to support up to 6,000 special education teachers, paraprofessionals and other related staff. *(See state-by-state estimates in the appendix.)* Because states are required by law to ensure that a free and appropriate public education is made available to all students with disabilities, these cuts in effect shift the burden for meeting the needs of children with disabilities to states and local communities.

Figure 1: Head Start Enrollment, 2000-2016
Thousands of slots

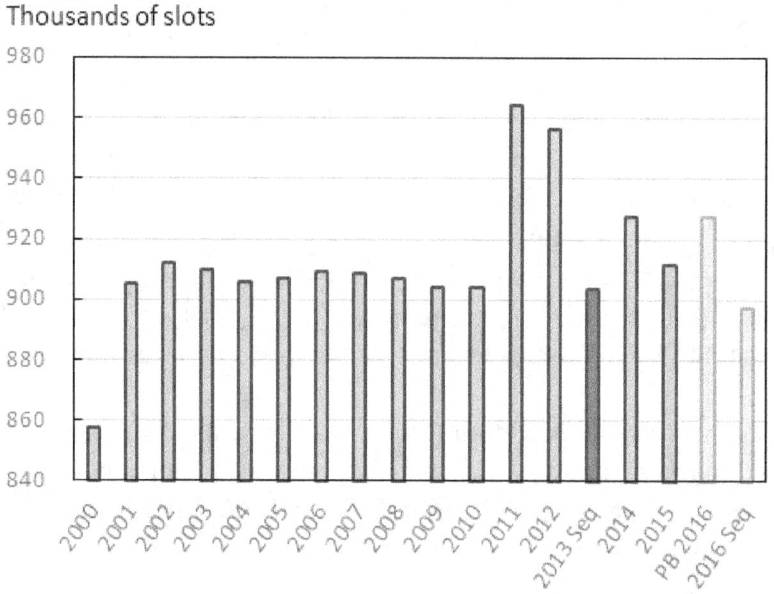

*Note: In addition to the slots displayed here, the American Recovery and Reinvestment Act of 2009 (P.L. 111-5) increased slots by 61,078 over FY 2009-10.*

**Job Training and Employment Services.** Last year, Congress came together to pass the first bipartisan job training reauthorization legislation in a decade, enacting the Workforce Innovation and Opportunity Act (WIOA). WIOA makes important improvements to the Nation's job training system, a critically important step in transforming the Nation's workforce system to meet the needs of a changing economy and better reflect the needs of job seekers and employers. But the accomplishments of WIOA reauthorization would be put at risk by the deep cuts required under the Republican budget levels.

When sequestration cuts took effect in 2013, 1.3 million people lost access to Department of Labor job training and employment services. In 2016, sequestration funding levels would mean 2.2 million fewer people would receive job training and employment services, including help finding jobs and skills training, as compared to the President's Budget. *(See state-by-state estimates in the appendix.)* Not only would the President's Budget serve more people, it would also scale up proven training and re-employment approaches, including apprenticeships, reemployment and eligibility assessments and reemployment services for jobless workers, and the Jobs-Plus program that has been found to help public housing residents succeed in the job market.

## Research and Development

Our long-term economic competitiveness depends upon continued investment in research and development (R&D) — from the basic research that has the potential to drive the great discoveries of the 21st century, to agricultural research focused on climate resilience and sustainability, to investments in developing advanced manufacturing technology.

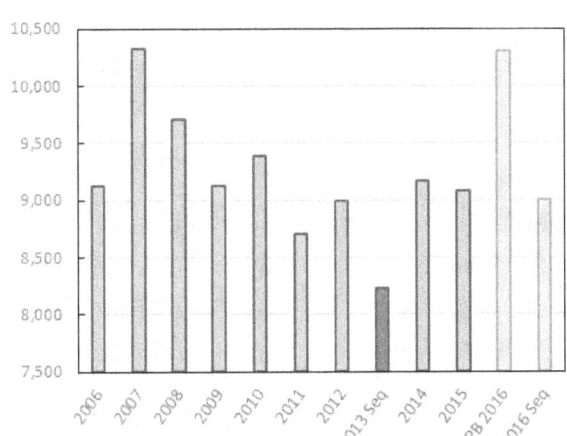

Figure 2a: NIH Competitive Grants Awarded, 2006-2016

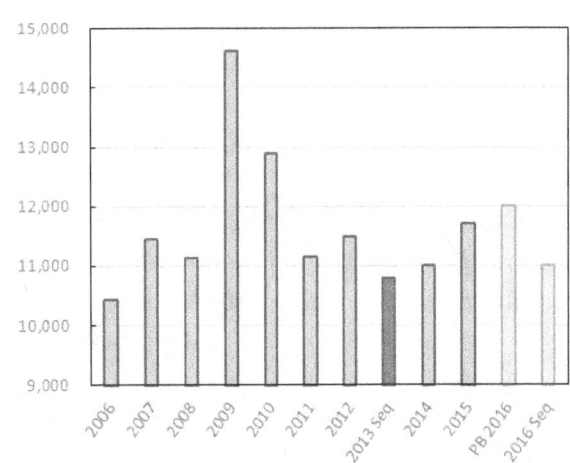

Figure 2b: NSF Competitive Awards Funded, 2006-2016

When sequestration took effect in 2013, it sharply curtailed federal support for health care research, with NIH awarding fewer new medical research grants than in any year since 1998 (see Figure 2). A return to sequestration funding levels in 2016 would bring the federal government's support for research to its lowest real level since 2002, with the exception of under the 2013 sequestration. Compared to the President's Budget, that would mean:

- More than $1 billion less in funding for **NIH**, translating into 1,300 fewer new grants and adversely impacting research across all disease areas. Sequestration funding levels could also squeeze out new initiatives proposed in the President's Budget, such as a major investment in Precision Medicine, an innovative approach to disease prevention which takes into account individual differences in people's genes, environments, and lifestyles to give clinicians the tools to better understand the complex mechanisms underlying a patient's condition and the ability to better predict which treatments will be effective. Other programs that could be cut include the Administration's BRAIN initiative, which is helping to revolutionize our understanding of the human brain and uncovering new ways to treat, prevent, and cure brain disorders like Alzheimer's, schizophrenia, autism, epilepsy, and traumatic brain injury.

- 950 fewer research grants at the **National Science Foundation (NSF)**, affecting about 11,600 researchers, technicians, and students. This reduction will slow the pace of discovery across fields of science and engineering – including areas like advanced manufacturing, clean energy, cybersecurity, and neuroscience – inhibiting research essential to U.S. innovation and economic competitiveness.

- An underinvestment in critical applied research, such as **manufacturing institutes** that bring companies, universities, community colleges, and federal agencies in a region together to bridge the gap between basic research and product development. When Congress came together on a bipartisan basis to partially reverse sequestration in 2014, the higher funding levels made room for investment in seven new manufacturing institutes, bringing the total to nine. The President's Budget proposes an additional seven new institutes in 2016 and would attain the goal of 45 institutes within ten years, but that expansion would be at risk at sequestration levels. In addition, the House Republican budget specifically proposes to eliminate the Hollings Manufacturing Extension Program, which provides critical technical and financial assistance for small manufacturers.

- Dramatic reductions of $838 million, or over 30 percent, to the Department of Energy's **Office of Energy Efficiency and Renewable Energy.** These reductions would significantly reduce the number of clean energy research, development, and demonstration projects supported in cooperation with industry, universities, and the national labs.

- Lower base funding for R&D at the **Department of Defense (DOD).** Federal R&D investments are supported within both the defense and non-defense budgets. DOD has a long history of funding both basic and applied research with national security applications, from stealth technology to GPS. Strengthening the nation's scientific and technical capabilities requires a balanced approach to reversing sequestration.

## Housing Assistance and Homelessness

Like other cuts in the Republican budget, maintaining sequestration funding levels for 2016 would disproportionately affect the most vulnerable Americans, and it would set back the progress we are making in tackling critical problems like homelessness.

Although chronic homelessness was long considered an intractable problem, a broad body of research has demonstrated that permanent supportive housing is both more effective at reducing chronic homelessness and more cost effective than traditional approaches – for instance, resulting in reduced hospitalization and emergency room visits. In 2010, the President set ambitious goals to end homelessness across the Nation, including ending homelessness among veterans in 2015. The President's Budgets have consistently requested the resources needed to meet homelessness reduction goals, and where Congress has provided those resources, we have made great progress. In particular, the total number of veterans experiencing homelessness has declined by 33 percent since 2010, and the number of unsheltered homeless veterans has declined by 43 percent (see Figure 3).

But despite the best efforts of states, local communities, and non-profit partners, our progress on ending homelessness for other populations – the chronically homeless, families and youth – has fallen behind due to insufficient funding, and was set back by the 2013 sequestration. Due to sequestration, an estimated 60,000 fewer individuals were served through the HUD Homeless Assistance Grants than were served in the previous year. Funding increased after Congress partially reversed sequestration for 2014 and 2015, but not enough to make up for lost ground, forcing the Administration to push back its timelines for ending chronic homelessness from 2015 to 2017.

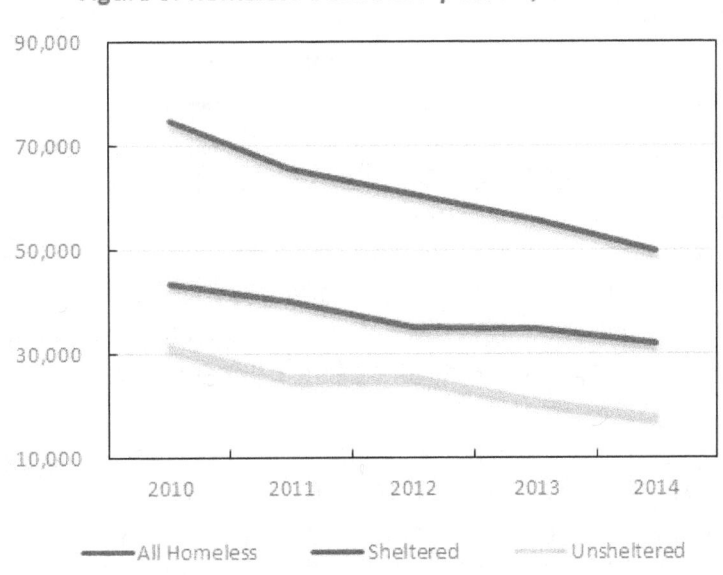

Figure 3: Homeless Veterans by Status, 2010-2014

The House Republican budget claims to share the Administration's goal of ending chronic homelessness. But the truth is, compared to the President's Budget, the Republican budget funding levels would leave thousands of individuals and families homeless. The Republican budgets would support at least 15,000 fewer families with rapid rehousing, at least 25,500 fewer units of permanent supportive housing targeted to the chronically homeless, and 62,000 fewer special-purpose vouchers, which would provide needed housing assistance to families, veterans, and tribal families experiencing homelessness, victims of domestic or dating violence, youth aging out of foster care, and families with children in the foster care system for whom assistance could facilitate reunification. All told, this means a needless delay in helping families and achieving an important national goal.

Sequestration funding levels would also impact other housing assistance programs. Compared to the President's Budget, the Republican budgets would:

- Serve approximately 133,000 fewer very low-income families with **Housing Choice Vouchers,** which help low-income families afford decent and safe housing in the private market. *(See state-by-state estimates in the appendix.)*

- Result in the loss of affordable rental housing for <u>20,000 rural families and elderly or disabled households</u>, many of whom depend on the **USDA's Rural Housing Service rental assistance program** to be able to remain in their homes.

## Cuts to Services for Seniors and People with Disabilities

Sequestration funding levels would also harm vulnerable populations, including the elderly and people with disabilities. For example, compared to the President's Budget, the Republican budgets' sequestration funding levels would cut **Home and Community-Based Supportive Services,** which could result in approximately <u>500,000 fewer rides to doctors and grocery stores</u>, <u>200,000 fewer hours of assistance to seniors</u> unable to perform activities of daily living, <u>and 100,000 fewer hours of care for dependent adults</u> in supervised, protective group settings.

## Public Health, Safety, and Other Core Functions of Government

The government has a fundamental responsibility to ensure the public's health and safety, and discretionary funding is essential to meeting this commitment. The President's Budget makes a number of key investments to strengthen the Nation's public health system and reform programs to improve public safety. Compared to the President's Budget, the Republican budget funding levels would:

- Damage **Federal and state law enforcement** efforts, resulting in more than <u>400 fewer Federal agents</u> to combat violent crime, pursue financial crimes, and ensure national security; <u>nearly 200 fewer Assistant U.S. Attorneys</u>; and <u>more than 300 fewer prison guards</u> to maintain the safe and secure confinement of inmates in federal prisons. Reductions to Federal grants would result in more than <u>600 fewer officer positions at the state and local level</u>, and a reduction of this magnitude could also damage bipartisan efforts to reduce recidivism.

  These and other security and safety investments that are funded as part of the non-defense budget underscore the importance of a balanced approach to reversing sequestration for protecting the American people.

- Result in <u>3,000 fewer patients</u> receiving critical antiretroviral treatments through the **Ryan White HIV/AIDS Program**, and <u>cutting almost 80,000 medical visits at Ryan White clinics</u>.

- Require the **Indian Health Service** to reduce current services, <u>resulting in 3,500 fewer inpatient and approximately 100,000 fewer outpatient visits</u>, despite the fact that the population for these services only continues to grow.

14

- Reduce the number of inspections the **Environmental Protection Agency (EPA)** can conduct for non-compliance with environmental laws to protect the water we drink and the air we breathe, delay criminal enforcement actions for polluters, postpone efforts to save taxpayer dollars by consolidating its facilities, and decrease support for state and tribal partners in their implementation of the Nation's environmental laws to protect the public's health.

## Infrastructure

The President's Budget outlines the Administration's plan to devote one-time revenue raised from the international tax reform component of pro-growth business tax reform plan to infrastructure investment, funding a six-year Surface Transportation Reauthorization and ensuring the solvency of the **Highway Trust Fund.** While the Republican budgets claim to support solvency, they allocate no resources and provide no plan to achieve this goal. Instead, they just establish vague reserve funds to, in the words of the House Budget, "provide for innovative thinking." Supported by the Highway Trust Fund, in FY 2014 the Federal Government obligated $39.5 billion to states through the Federal Aid Highways program for highway planning and construction and over $11.1 billion through Transit Formula Grants that support our Nation's mass transit systems. *(See state-by-state estimates in the appendix.)*

Meanwhile, while the President's Budget proposes to permanently authorize the competitive **TIGER** grant program to spur innovation, create jobs, and promote resilient infrastructure in communities across the Nation, the Republican budget funding levels could result in cuts to TIGER at a time when demand from states and local communities for transportation investment far outstrips the available funding.

Beyond the Department of Transportation, other agencies also have important infrastructure responsibilities that would be shortchanged by the Republican budgets. For example:

- The **National Park Service** is responsible for maintaining America's parks and historic sites and preserving our unique cultural and historical identity. While the President's Budget celebrates the centennial anniversary of our great parks with an historic investment in enhancing park services and upgrading and restoring park facilities, the Republican budgets' cuts would force some park managers to shorten visitor hours, reduce seasonal hiring, and further increase the maintenance backlog. The Republican budget funding levels would cut funding for 26 of 35 construction projects and 208 of 464 rehabilitation projects proposed in the President's Budget. *(See map below and appendix for state-by-state impacts on construction and repair & rehabilitation projects.)*

- The Department of Energy's **Weatherization Assistance Program** has improved the lives of more than 7 million families by reducing their energy bills through grants to states to provide weatherization services to those in need using the latest technologies for home energy upgrades. The Republican budgets would result in approximately 3,500 fewer low-income residential retrofits next year, forgoing annual per unit average energy cost savings of $250-480 per year over the next two decades.

**National Security**

As a wide range of national security experts ranging from former Secretary of Defense Robert Gates to Ambassador John Bolton have pointed out, locking in sequestration for defense would undermine our readiness and efforts to secure technological superiority for U.S. forces in future conflicts. It would ultimately result in a military that is too small and insufficiently equipped to fully implement the Nation's defense strategy, thereby damaging our national security and breaking faith with our service members.

Under 2013 sequestration, the Department of Defense endured deep cuts to readiness, weathered civilian pay freezes and furloughs, and cut badly needed investments in modernization and critical technologies. 650,000 DOD employees were furloughed for six days. The Navy was forced to cancel deployment for five ships. The Air Force grounded 31 flying squadrons. The Army canceled its capstone training exercise for seven Brigade Combat Teams.

A return to sequestration funding levels in 2016 would bring real defense funding to its lowest level since 2006. In the near term, this undermines our readiness and efforts to secure technological superiority for U.S. forces in future conflicts. The Army would shrink by 60,000 soldiers, beyond already-planned reductions of 150,000 from its peak size in 2011. The Marine Corps would have to cut two infantry battalions and shrink from 182,000 Marines to 175,000, after having already reduced from a peak of 202,000 Marines in 2011. The Navy would cut its carrier fleet from 11 to 10. The Air Force would be forced to reduce the number of around-the-clock surveillance patrols it can conduct from 60 to 50. Sequestration would also disrupt acquisition programs, defer equipment maintenance, cancel training, decrease procurement, and slow the development and testing of new technologies.

Instead of lifting sequestration, the Republican budgets try to have it both ways on defense funding – maintaining sequestration and then using overseas contingency operations (OCO) funds intended for wars and not subject to budget caps to fund the day-to-day operations of the Pentagon. Leaders in both parties have acknowledged how irresponsible this is. Former House Budget Chairman Paul Ryan referred to it as treating overseas contingency funding as a "slush fund," and Senators Mike Crapo and Jeff Flake just last week called it a "gimmick."

The Federal budget should clearly articulate policy priorities and provide a strategic, credible, and responsible investment plan to fund them. This allows the American people to have an informed debate about where to invest, avoids surprise costs, and enables the military to fully execute a long-term strategy. Instead of providing clarity, the Republicans' OCO gimmick blurs the distinction between what costs are from overseas contingencies, and what costs are for day-to-day operations. And by relying on a dramatic one-time OCO increase to pay for basic defense costs, the OCO gimmick does not realistically fund ongoing defense requirements. The Republican budgets provide a one-time OCO increase of nearly $40 billion in 2016, but the Senate provides no credible mechanism to avoid returning to sequestration levels the following years, and the House resorts to slashing non-defense funding dramatically to sustain its defense increase.

The military must have long-term budget stability, not one-off increases that create uncertainty and undermine strategic planning. Chairman of the Joint Chiefs of Staff General Martin Dempsey has said that funding DOD's base budget is critical to providing the certainty the Pentagon needs to operate, telling Congress "My advice is that we need to fix our base budget, because you build the institution through the base budget, and you respond to contingencies with the fund called [Overseas] Contingency Operations." Likewise, Defense Secretary Ash Carter told Congress, "[I]t is the base [budget] upon which we build our future budgets. And we need stability... Otherwise, we can't spend it efficiently, and we can't spend it strategically."

In contrast to the Republican budgets, the President's Budget is clear, realistic, and strategic. It makes long-term investments above the sequestration levels to restore military readiness over the next several years, and responsibly funds recapitalization and modernization programs needed to ensure our continued technological edge. Unlike the Republican budgets, it does not pretend that sequestration is acceptable for our defense strategy by circumventing it using budget gimmicks. It provides financial stability and realistic cost estimates and financing mechanisms instead of subjecting the military to the uncertainty of a one-year planning horizon without stable multi-year funding. And it recognizes that our Nation can only sustain a strong military if it invests in a strong economy, which is accomplished through needed investments in the educational system, business, and research.

Beyond the military, the Republican budgets' implications for international assistance programs are severe, reducing U.S. contributions to peacekeeping operations by over a quarter relative to the President's Budget. If a cut of this magnitude was applied directly to ongoing UN missions, it would translate into <u>9,783 fewer peacekeepers</u> in some of the most vulnerable parts of the world, and would reduce the number of personnel to protect civilians, maintain peace and security, assist in disarmament, demobilize and reintegrate of former combatants, support the organization of elections, protect and promote human rights, and assist in restoring rule of law.

Even Deeper Cuts to Pro-Growth Discretionary Investments in Later Years

Both the House and Senate Republican budgets would cut key pro-growth investments even more deeply after 2016, but they take different approaches.

The Senate budget would cut non-defense discretionary investments by almost 5 percent below sequestration levels between 2017-2025. Meanwhile, it would keep sequestration in place for defense, with increasingly serious consequences for national security. The long-term consequences of sequestration for the military would be hard-hitting, requiring a reassessment of our strategic approach to addressing the threats we face. If sequestration persists over the long term, Secretary Carter has said the cuts will require a reassessment of our strategic approach to global threats, with the military prepared to do significantly less than what the American public currently expects of it.

The House budget would increase defense funding above sequestration after 2016 – but only at the expense of doubling and then tripling its cuts to education and training, research, public safety, and other non-defense priorities. The budget hides these deep cuts in later years to mask their effects. But if non-defense discretionary funding were cut 12 percent below sequestration levels in 2016 – the cut the House Republican budget would make in 2018 – it would mean the following compared to the President's Budget:

- More than 157,000 children would lose out on access to Head Start services.
- More than 4 million workers would lose out on job training and employment services.
- Title I education funding would be $2.7 billion lower, enough to fund about 10,000 schools, 38,000 teachers, and aides, and 4.2 million students.
- IDEA funding would be nearly $1.6 billion lower, an amount that could support up to 26,800 special education teachers, paraprofessionals, and other related staff.
- Research funding at NIH would fall to its lowest level since 2002.
- HUD's Housing Choice Voucher program would likely serve approximately 350,000-400,000 fewer very low-income families.

Cutting Aid to the Most Vulnerable and Programs that Help Low-Income Children and Families Succeed

The Republican budgets target programs for low- and moderate-income families for deep cuts, increasing poverty and closing off key pathways to opportunity for low-income children, students who need help going to college, and workers who need to upgrade their skills to make it in today's global economy.

The budget resolutions would make unprecedented cuts to key areas, including:

- **Supplemental Nutrition Assistance Program (SNAP):** The House Republican budget would convert SNAP to a block grant and cut funding by about $125 billion over the 2021-2025 period, jeopardizing nutrition assistance for the more than 46 million Americans who depend on it, the majority of whom are children, seniors, and people with disabilities. Over the five year period, the House would cut funding by about one-third. That is the equivalent of cutting 11 to 12 million people off the program entirely, or, if benefits were cut across-the-board, the equivalent of cutting benefits by an average of $55 per person per month, dollars families use to put food on the table.[6] The Senate budget provides less specificity but appears to

---

[6] "House Budget Would Slash SNAP by $125 Billion Over Ten Years." Dorothy Rosenbaum and Brynne Keith-Jennings. Center on Budget and Policy Priorities, March 2015: http://www.cbpp.org/cms/index.cfm?fa=view&id=5287.

include SNAP cuts that are at least as large as those in the House budget. *(See state-by-state estimates in the appendix.)*

- **Pell Grants:** The House Republican budget calls for freezing Pell Grants for the next decade, allowing them to erode with inflation and provide less and less help to students. This would make it harder for the more than 8 million students who now use Pell Grants to help pay for college. But the budget goes even further. It eliminates more than $90 billion in funding over 10 years for Pell Grants, calling into question whether the funding would be available to provide even its reduced Pell Grant levels. *(See state-by-state estimates in the appendix.)*

- **Federal Student Loan Repayment:** The House Republican budget assumes significant cuts to core student loan repayment programs that help Americans manage their debt responsibly. The House Budget calls for rolling back recent expansions of income-based repayment plans, which will hurt millions of borrowers by raising their monthly payments. In addition, the budget would end public service loan forgiveness – doubling the amount of time many teachers, nurses, and those in military service will need to finish paying their student loans.

- **Tax Credits for Working Families:** As discussed further below, the Republican budgets do nothing to prevent a tax increase on 26 million working families and students. The Earned Income Tax Credit, the Child Tax Credit, and the American Opportunity Tax Credit all help low- and moderate-income working families lower their tax bills, make ends meet, and in the case of the AOTC, pay for college. If improvements to these tax credits expire after 2017, as would occur under the Republican budgets, a mother with two children who works full-time at the minimum wage would lose more than $1,700. *(See state-by-state estimates in the appendix.)*

- **Massive unspecified cuts in budget areas that provide critical assistance to low-income Americans.** Both Republican budgets include hundreds of billions in unspecified cuts in the budget category that funds key supports for low-income Americans including[7]:

  o Supplemental Security Income, which provides assistance to poor seniors and people with disabilities;
  o Child nutrition programs, such as school lunch;
  o Child care subsidies that helps low-income families afford care so they can work and supports healthy child development and early learning;
  o Funding for welfare-to-work programs through the Temporary Assistance for Needy families program;
  o Unemployment Insurance benefits for jobless workers.

These cuts, along with cuts in key discretionary programs such as Head Start, housing assistance, and job training, would increase poverty and hardship. Moreover, they would also close off paths to opportunity for children, students, and workers. For example:

---

[7] This budget category, known as Income Security, also includes civil service and military retirement benefits.

- SNAP[8] and tax credits[9] such as the EITC have been shown not only to reduce child poverty but also to have a positive impact on children's educational attainment and, thus, their future earnings.
- Health coverage for children, critical to their development and future prospects, is threatened by a Medicaid block grant and massive funding cuts.[10]
- Early learning, supported by Head Start, public preschool, and child care, would be cut, jeopardizing school readiness and future education success.[11]
- Housing assistance helps families maintain stable housing and helps families move to communities with greater opportunities, including neighborhoods with better schools.
- A postsecondary degree or credential is one of the best paths to the middle class. College graduates earn more[12] and have higher employment rates[13] than those with only a high school degree, but cutting Pell Grants restricts access to college, making it harder for students to reach the middle class fulfill their full potential.
- Tax credits for working parents and child care are important work supports that boost employment among parents, helping them get and keep jobs and provide for their families.[14]

---

[8] "Long Run Impacts of Childhood Access to the Safety Net." Hilary W. Hoynes, Diane Whitmore Schanzenbach, and Douglas Almond. National Bureau of Economic Research, November 2012: http://www.nber.org/papers/w18535.

[9] "EITC and Child Tax Credit Promote Work, Reduce Poverty, and Support Children's Development, Research Finds." Chuck Marr, Chye-Ching Huang, Arloc Sherman, and Brandon DeBot. Center on Budget and Policy Priorities, March 2015: http://www.cbpp.org/cms/index.cfm?fa=view&id=3793#_ftn29.

[10] "The Effect of Child Health Insurance Access on Schooling: Evidence from Public Insurance Expansions." Cohodes et al. National Bureau of Economic Research, May 2014.

[11] "The Economics of Early Childhood Investments." The President's Council of Economic Advisors, December 2014/January 2015: https://www.whitehouse.gov/sites/default/files/docs/early_childhood_report1.pdf.

[12] "USUAL WEEKLY EARNINGS OF WAGE AND SALARY WORKERS FOURTH QUARTER 2014." U.S. Bureau of Labor Statistics, January 2015: http://www.bls.gov/news.release/archives/wkyeng_01212015.pdf.

[13] "HOUSEHOLD DATA, SEASONALLY ADJUSTED. A-5. Employment status of the civilian noninstitutional population 25 years and over by educational attainment, seasonally adjusted." U.S. Bureau of Labor Statistics: http://www.bls.gov/cps/cpsaat07.pdf

[14] Council of Economic Advisors (2014) and Marr (2015).

## II. Health Policy: The President's Plan to Build on the Affordable Care Act's Success Versus Republican Proposals to Cut Coverage and End Medicare as We Know It

On March 23, 2010 President Obama signed the Affordable Care Act (ACA) into law. The enactment of this legislation came after nearly 100 years of effort to advance comprehensive health care reform in the United States. Five years later, the Affordable Care Act is working. Thanks to its coverage provisions, the share of Americans without health insurance is at historic lows (see Figure 4). Americans are getting affordable coverage, with nearly eight in ten HealthCare.gov consumers finding coverage options costing $100 or less after tax credits, and without worrying about being denied coverage for pre-existing conditions. The ACA has expanded coverage for preventive services, including vaccines, cancer screenings, and birth control, at no out-of-pocket cost. Ensuring everyone has access to affordable health coverage will cost the government almost one-third less than the Congressional Budget Office (CBO) initially projected. And thanks in part to provisions of the Affordable Care that align payments with costs and deploy payment models that encourage more efficient, higher-quality care, we have seen a historic slowdown in the growth of health care costs, alongside striking improvements in the quality of care patients receive.

**Figure 4: Share of Population without Health Insurance, 1963-2015:Q1**

Source: CEA analysis of NHIS; ASPE analysis of NHIS and Gallup-Healthways Well-Being Index data through March 4, 2015; CEA calculations.
Note: Data are quarterly starting in 2014:Q1. Data for earlier years are generally either annual or bi-annual. The NHIS is the best tool for studying trends in insurance coverage, but because NHIS data are not currently available after 2014:Q2, Gallup data are used to extrapolate the uninsured rate through 2015:Q1.

But almost exactly five years after the ACA was enacted into law, Congressional Republicans will be voting for the more than 50th time to repeal these provisions. Not only that, but the House Republican budget proposes to block grant Medicaid and slash its funding by more than $900 billion, jeopardizing coverage for millions more Americans. The ACA has driven the largest decline in the uninsured rate since the decade following the creation of Medicare and Medicaid. Not only would the House Republican budget reverse those gains, it could produce the sharpest increase in the uninsured rate the Nation has ever seen and would double the number of uninsured Americans. Insurers would once again be able to discriminate against people with pre-existing conditions, and millions of seniors and people with disabilities would lose help paying for their prescription drugs. Meanwhile, rather than strengthening Medicare through smart reforms that encourage better, more efficient care, the House budget would end Medicare as we know it by replacing guaranteed access to the traditional Medicare program with a voucher program, increasing costs and forcing millions of seniors out of traditional Medicare.

## The President's Plan

The President's plan builds on the success of the ACA to continue expanding coverage and improving health care quality, while containing costs. The President's Budget:

- Fully funds the ongoing implementation of the ACA's health insurance coverage improvements through the operation of Health Insurance Marketplaces.
- Strengthens Medicare by more closely aligning payments with the costs of providing care, encouraging health care providers to deliver better care and better outcomes for their patients, and improving access to care for beneficiaries.
- Lowers drug costs for Medicare beneficiaries, closing the Medicare Part D donut hole for brand drugs by 2017, rather than 2020, by increasing discounts from the pharmaceutical industry.
- Strengthens Medicaid, providing affordable health coverage and economic security for the Nation's seniors and low-income working Americans and families, and preserves the Children's Health Insurance Program (CHIP), which currently serves over eight million children of working parents who are not eligible for Medicaid.
- Makes strategic investments in our Nation's health care workforce to ensure rural communities and other underserved populations have access to doctors and other providers, and serves approximately 28.6 million patients at more than 9,000 health center sites in medically underserved communities throughout the country.
- Supports the Administration's push to improve the Nation's health care delivery system. That means avoiding costly mistakes and readmissions, rewarding quality instead of quantity, and creating the health information technology infrastructure that enables new payment and delivery models to work.

## The Congressional Republican Approach

### Undoing Progress from the Affordable Care Act

The ACA is working, but in the same week as its fifth anniversary, Congressional Republicans will be voting for the more than 50th time to repeal its provisions. After five years of the Affordable Care Act, more than 16 million people have gained health coverage, and the

Nation's uninsured rate has reached historic lows. The House Budget Resolution would repeal all of the improvements in the ACA, eliminating coverage options for the millions of Americans who have obtained coverage through the Marketplaces, through Medicaid, or through a parent's plan. In addition to taking away Americans' health care security, the significant steps the ACA has taken to bend the healthcare cost curve and slow down cost growth could be put in jeopardy, potentially raising costs for families and businesses.

Repealing the ACA would:

- Eliminate Marketplace coverage for the 11.7 million Americans who have newly signed up or been re-enrolled in coverage for 2015, and for millions more who have gained coverage due to the ACA Medicaid expansion. Many of these individuals would become uninsured, while others would end up with worse or less affordable coverage. *(See state-by-state estimates in the appendix.)*
- Deprive up to 130 million Americans with pre-existing conditions of the security of knowing they will still be able to buy affordable health coverage if they lose their jobs or otherwise lose their health insurance;
- Eliminate coverage for millions of young adults who gained coverage through a parent's plan, a crucial option for young adults who wish to stay in school or take a job without health coverage; and;
- Increase prescription drug costs for more than 5 million seniors and people with disabilities. *(See state-by-state estimates in the appendix.)*

**Figure 5: Adult Uninsured Rates, 1997-2014:Q2**

Source: National Health Interview Survey; CEA calculations.

23

## Endangering Medicare and Increasing Costs for Seniors

This year will mark the 50th anniversary of the enactment of Medicare and Medicaid. Medicare has long provided affordable health coverage to support longer, healthier lives and economic security for the Nation's seniors and people with disabilities. Today, Medicare provides about 55 million Americans with dependable medical insurance. But whereas the President's Budget proposes to strengthen and preserve Medicare through reforms that encourage high-quality and efficient care, the House Republican budget would end Medicare as we know it by replacing guaranteed access to the traditional Medicare program with a voucher program, increasing costs for millions of seniors and risking a death spiral as private plans siphon off healthier and less expensive beneficiaries. The House Republican budget would:

- **Risk increased health care costs for millions of seniors.** For new beneficiaries starting in 2024, the House Republican budget would replace guaranteed access to the traditional Medicare program with a voucher program. Beneficiaries would receive a premium-support payment that may not completely offset the premium for the Medicare plan of their choice (either a private plan or the traditional Medicare program), potentially increasing health care costs for millions of seniors who depend on Medicare.

- **Force millions of seniors out of traditional Medicare and risk an adverse selection death spiral.** As CBO and numerous outside analysts have found, under a voucher system healthier, lower-cost Medicare beneficiaries would be more likely to enroll in private plans. Because traditional Medicare would be left with sicker, more expensive beneficiaries, it would have to charge higher premiums than private plans to recover costs. Traditional Medicare has been the leader in reforming the health care system to improve efficiency, but its ability to contain costs would be limited in a premium support system. Both of these factors would make traditional Medicare an unaffordable option for more and more beneficiaries, resulting in escalating costs and potentially even a "death spiral" in which traditional Medicare could become unaffordable in parts of the country.

## Slashing Medicaid

Medicaid is critically important to providing health care coverage to millions of the neediest Americans, including low-income children, people with disabilities, and seniors receiving long term services and supports. Both the House and Senate Republican budgets would sharply cut Medicaid and Children's Health Insurance Program (CHIP) funding to states, resulting in states having to either contribute a greater share to continue their programs at current levels or make significant cuts, such as reductions in program eligibility levels, cuts to provider reimbursement rates, reductions in benefits for those currently enrolled, and cost-shifts to beneficiaries. Both budgets would also repeal the Affordable Care Act, including the option for states to expand their Medicaid programs with enhanced Federal support, resulting in millions more losing coverage.

- Over the next decade, the House Republican Budget would cut Medicaid funding to states by more than $900 billion, resulting in a cut of more than 20 percent of projected Medicaid spending over the next ten years. *(See state-by-state estimates in the appendix.)*

- Approximately $800 billion would be cut from Medicaid nation-wide due to the repeal of the ACA Medicaid expansion. To date, 28 states and the District of Columbia have taken up this option, expanding coverage to millions who were previously uninsured.

- A Kaiser Family Foundation analysis of previous House budget resolutions that included a Medicaid block grant proposal found as many as 20 million people would be denied the coverage they would have gotten under the pre-ACA Medicaid.

- Cuts of this magnitude would inevitably mean that many seniors and persons with disabilities would experience disruption in care and financial hardship. According to the Kaiser Family Foundation, in 2010, of the Nation's 1.4 million residents in certified nursing home facilities, Medicaid was the primary payer for 63 percent, Medicare was the primary payer for 14 percent, and private and other coverage was the source for 22 percent.

## III. Tax Policy: The President's Plan to Close Loopholes and Expand Opportunity for the Middle Class Versus Republican Proposals to Provide another High-Income Tax Cut

Nowhere is the contrast between the President's Budget and the Republican budgets more vivid than with respect to tax policy. In his Fiscal Year 2016 Budget, the President proposes to simplify our tax code, make it fairer by eliminating some of the largest tax loopholes, and reinvest the savings in measures that will grow the economy and expand opportunity. The President's plan would make paychecks go further in covering the cost of child care, college, and a secure retirement. It would also create and improve tax credits that support and reward work. (See Table 1.)

These proposals would be fully paid for, primarily by closing the "trust fund loophole," increasing the top capital gains and dividend tax rate to 28 percent, and imposing a fee on large, highly leveraged financial institutions. In addition, the President takes a balanced approach to deficit reduction that would put the Nation's finances on a sustainable fiscal path by obtaining $1.8 trillion in deficit reduction through a mix of tax, health, and immigration reforms.

The budgets being debated this week by House and Senate Republicans take a very different approach – one that promises large tax cuts to millionaires, fails to invest in middle-class families, and does nothing to prevent a tax increase on millions of working families and students. Most important, Congressional Republicans are unwilling to close a single tax loophole to help reduce the deficit. As a result, the entire burden of deficit reduction under their budgets falls on the middle-class, seniors, low-income children and families, and national security, with the consequences for growth, opportunity, health, and safety described above.

| Table 1: Tax Policy in the President's Budget Versus the Congressional Republican Budgets | |
|---|---|
| **President's Budget** | **Congressional Republican Budgets** |
| Cuts taxes for middle-class families paying for child care, putting kids through college, and saving for retirement | Specified tax policies (House) are targeted toward the wealthy and corporations and provide millionaires with tax cuts averaging $50,000 |
| Strengthens EITC and continues EITC and Child Tax Credit (CTC) improvements vital to working families | Do nothing to prevent tax increase averaging $900 on 16 million families from expiration of EITC and CTC improvements |
| Expands and makes permanent the American Opportunity Tax Credit (AOTC) to help families and students afford college | Do nothing to prevent the AOTC from expiring, letting 12 million families paying for college lose tax credits worth $1,100 on average |
| Pays for major investments in infrastructure through detailed proposals to reform the business tax system | No plan for addressing looming Highway Trust Fund solvency or investing in infrastructure |
| Fiscally responsible, balanced approach that closes loopholes and asks the wealthy to pay their fair share | Do not identify a single tax loophole to close or ask the wealthy to contribute a dollar to deficit reduction, putting full burden on the middle-class, seniors, low-income families, and national security |

**Making Child Care, Education, and Retirement Tax Benefits Work for Middle-Class Families**

- **A simplified and dramatically expanded child care credit**. Access to affordable, high-quality child care and early education promotes child development and helps support parents who are struggling to balance work and family obligations. Yet access is too often limited by high and rising costs, and child care is now the largest single expense families face throughout much of the country. The President's plan helps working families by simplifying and expanding child care tax benefits, including by tripling the maximum child care tax credit for children under 5 (to up to $3,000 per child) and making the full credit available to most middle-class families. These proposals would benefit 5.1 million families, helping them cover child care costs for 6.7 million children (including 3.5 million children under 5). The Budget also provides $82 billion to make quality, affordable child care available to all eligible low-and moderate-income working families with young children through the Child Care and Development Fund (CCDF), expanding access to more than 1.1 million additional children under the age of four by 2025.

- **Education tax reform to simplify duplicative and confusing incentives and improve college affordability.** The President's higher education plan would consolidate a complicated set of education tax provisions into an improved American Opportunity Tax Credit (AOTC). The AOTC, which the President signed into law in 2009, provides a tax credit of up to $2,500 each year for up to four years of higher education. But it is set to expire after 2017. The President's Budget proposal makes the AOTC permanent and expands it in several ways. The Budget would allow the AOTC to be claimed over five years (for a maximum of $12,500 compared to $10,000 currently), increase the refundable portion, expand eligibility for part-time students, and adjust the AOTC for inflation in future years. The President's Budget includes additional reforms to education tax benefits that – together with the AOTC expansion – would cut taxes for 8.5 million working families and students by an average of $750, and simplify taxes for the more than 25 million families and students that claim education tax benefits.

- **Retirement tax reform that dramatically expands access to employer-based retirement savings options.** The President's Budget includes proposals to improve the retirement savings system for working Americans while closing loopholes and ensuring that retirement tax incentives serve their intended purpose of bolstering retirement security. Under the President's plan, 30 million additional American workers would have access to easy, payroll-based retirement savings. Specifically, the plan would provide for automatic IRA enrollment for millions of workers without access to a workplace retirement plan and strengthen tax credits for small employers that provide retirement savings options for their employees. The plan would also prevent wealthy individuals from using tax loopholes to accumulate millions of dollars of tax-favored retirement benefits.

**Reforming the Tax System to Better Support and Reward Work**

- **A new "second earner credit" for two-earner families.** The President's Budget builds on bipartisan proposals to address the unique challenges faced by two-earner couples by providing a "second-earner credit" of up to $500. The second-earner credit will help 24 million families meet the additional costs of having two spouses work, such as commuting, professional expenses, child care, and, increasingly, elder care.

- **An expanded childless worker EITC and permanent extension of the EITC and CTC improvements enacted in the Recovery Act.** The President's Budget strengthens the Earned Income Tax Credit (EITC) and Child Tax Credit (CTC), which reduce taxes for working families and increase labor force participation, by:

  - **Preventing a tax increase on 16 million working families.** Critical improvements to the EITC and CTC expire after 2017. If allowed to happen, this would raise taxes on 16 million working families by an average of $900. The President's Budget makes these improvements permanent.
  - **Expanding the EITC for workers without children.** The President's Budget proposes to significantly expand the EITC for workers without children and non-custodial parents. The proposal would directly reduce poverty and hardship for 13 million low-income workers while encouraging labor force participation among groups with low or declining participation rates. Expanding the "childless EITC" is an idea that has garnered bipartisan support (although House Budget Committee Republicans rejected an amendment that would have added it to their budget).

**Eliminating the Biggest Loopholes that Let the Wealthiest Avoid Paying Their Fair Share and Reforming Financial Sector Taxation**

The President's Budget would pay for the middle-class and pro-work reforms by eliminating tax loopholes for the wealthy and reforming the taxation of the financial sector. Despite rising income and wealth disparities over the past few decades, the tax system has changed in ways that make it easier for the wealthy to avoid paying their fair share. The tax system also favors income from wealth over income from work, with lower marginal tax rates on capital income, such as gains and dividends, and numerous loopholes. The President's Budget would:

- Eliminate the largest capital gains tax loophole: the "trust fund loophole" that allows the wealthy never to pay tax on capital gains on much of their assets.
- Restore the top rate on capital gains and dividends to 28 percent – the rate at which capital gains were taxed under President Reagan. That top rate would apply to couples with incomes of about $500,000 and above.
- Discourage risk-taking in the financial sector by imposing a fee on net liabilities of the roughly 100 largest U.S. financial firms, those with assets over $50 billion.

- Protect the Social Security and Medicare trust funds by closing a loophole allowing certain high-paid professionals to avoid paying Social Security and Medicare taxes.

## The Congressional Republican Approach

### Large Tax Cuts for High-Income Households and Corporations

In a budget that claims to be fiscally responsible, House Republicans start by promising large tax cuts for the wealthy and big corporations. Among the few specific tax proposals in the House Republican budget is a promise to spend hundreds of billions on high-income and business tax cuts.[15] The proposals they specify would cut the tax bill of the average millionaire by more than $50,000, before even adding the proposed cuts to tax rates.

Besides these tax cuts in the House budget, the Republican budgets provide few specifics on tax issues. This year's House budget calls for cutting individual and corporate rates but does not say what rates should be or give any detail as to how the Budget would make up the revenue. However, in recent years, Congressional Republicans have made clear that their top priority in tax reform is to cut the tax rates for the highest-income individuals. Recent House Republican budgets, for example, proposed lowering the highest individual rate by more than one-third, to the lowest level since the presidency of Herbert Hoover. Coupled with other tax policies, these top-bracket tax cuts were estimated to be so costly that meeting the GOP's proposed fiscal targets would require an average tax increase of $2,000 to $3,000 or more on families with children making less than $200,000.[16]

### Letting Taxes Rise for 26 Million Working Families and Students

Meanwhile, the House and Senate Republican budgets do nothing to prevent a tax increase on 26 million working families and students. At the end of 2017, unless Congress acts, several significant tax credit improvements signed into law by President Obama and extended twice on a bipartisan basis will expire. These expiring provisions include improvements to the Earned

---

[15] The only specified tax policies in the House GOP budget are (1) repealing the Affordable Care Act in its entirety, including the Net Investment Income Tax on high-income individuals and the 0.9% additional Medicare tax on high-income individuals, and (2) repealing the Alternative Minimum Tax, which is predominantly paid by upper-income individuals. Previous analyses by the Tax Policy Center suggest that repealing these provisions would cut taxes by about $50,000 for those with incomes over $1 million. Taxpayers earning between $50,000 and $75,000 would save an average of less than $10; those earning less than $50,000 would save essentially nothing. See Tax Policy center tables T14-0087 and T12-0108 and http://www.offthechartsblog.org/house-budget-chairs-priority-tax-cuts-for-well-to-do/.

[16] The nonpartisan Tax Policy Center analyzed a similar plan in 2012 – which cut the top individual rates to 28 percent, while the House GOP budget proposed to cut them to 25 percent – and found that even with generous assumptions, it would necessitate raising taxes on families with children and incomes under $200,000 by more than $2,000. Since the House Republican budget proposed deeper cuts, others estimated that it would necessitate raising taxes on middle-class families by even more – at least $3,000. See http://www.taxpolicycenter.org/publications/url.cfm?ID=1001628; http://www.cbpp.org/cms/?fa=view&id=3926.

Income Tax Credit (EITC) that benefit families with three or more children and reduce the EITC's so-called "marriage penalty" (when married couples receive smaller tax credits than they would if they were not married and filed taxes as single individuals). They also include improvements to the Child Tax Credit that allow low-wage workers count more of their earnings toward the credit's refundable portion. The American Opportunity Tax Credit that helps families afford the costs of higher education also expires after 2017.

As illustrated in Figures 6a and 6b, while the President's Budget invests in the middle class, the House and Senate Republican budgets do the opposite.

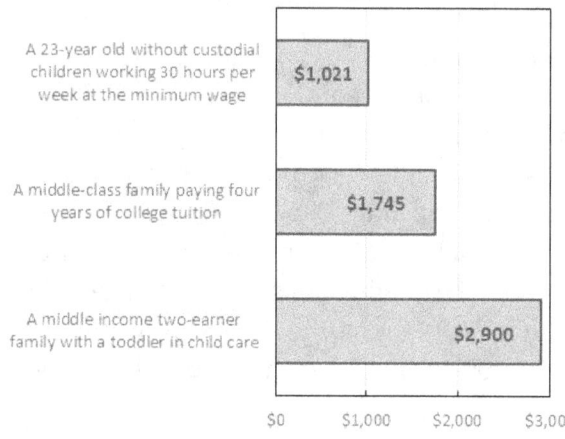

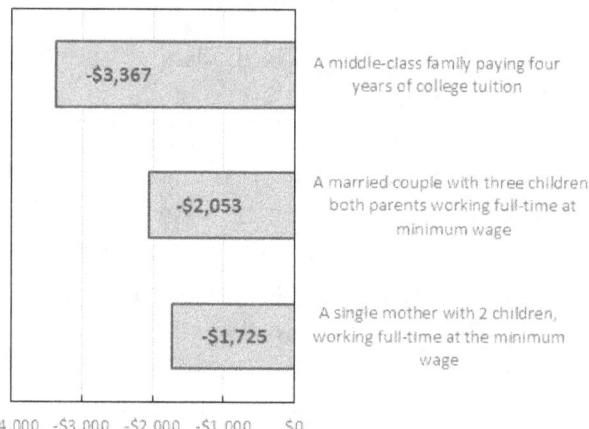

Source: Calculations based on U.S. Department of Treasury, U.S. Department of Education National Center for Education Statistics, and Center on Budget and Policy Priorities data.

Notes: Tax changes are calculated for illustrative families and are relative to current policy. Changes in education tax credits include the cumulative change over four academic years (tax years 2016-20), and assume the family pays median tuition and fees at a four-year public, non-doctoral university. All other tax changes under the President's Budget are for tax year 2016, and all other tax changes under the Republican Budgets are for tax year 2018. (Tax cuts under the President's Budget include the impact of proposed improvements to the childless EITC, AOTC, child and dependent care tax credit, and new second earner credit. Tax increases under the Republican budgets result from allowing the AOTC and improvements to the EITC and Child Tax Credit to expire after 2017.)

Both the House and Senate Republican budget fail to provide for extending these tax credits (and both assume the revenue from their expiration). If the EITC and CTC improvements are allowed to expire:

- 16 million working families would lose tax credits and effectively get a $900 pay cut, on average. *(See state-by-state estimates in the appendix.)*
- 16 million people would be pushed into poverty or deeper into poverty, including almost 8 million children.
- A full-time, minimum wage worker with two children would lose her entire Child Tax Credit of more than $1,700.

If the AOTC is allowed to expire:

- 12 million families and students paying for college would see their tuition tax credits reduced by an average of $1,100.
- The AOTC would revert to the less generous Hope credit, which would be available for only two years of higher education, compared to four years today and five years under the President's Budget.

In sum, allowing these tax cuts to expire would raise taxes on 26 million families by an average of about $1,000 each.[17]

## Does Not Ask the Wealthy or Corporations to Contribute a Dollar to Deficit Reduction

Finally, while the House Republican budget specifies tax policies that would give millionaires an average tax cut of $50,000, both it and the Senate Republican budget fail to identify a single tax loophole to close. Moreover, the Republican budgets are clear that if they did find any loopholes to close, the revenue would go toward reducing marginal tax rates or other new tax cuts – not reducing the deficit. Revenues would be kept at current baseline levels – necessarily putting the entire burden of deficit reduction on the middle-class, seniors, and low-income children and families.

---

[17] The 26 million families include some who would be affected by the expiration of the American Opportunity Tax Credit as well as the expiration of the EITC or CTC improvements.

# Appendix: State-by-State Estimates

## HEAD START [18]

| State | Fewer Children Served | State | Fewer Children Served |
|---|---|---|---|
| Alabama | 570 | Montana | 110 |
| Alaska | 70 | Nebraska | 200 |
| Arizona | 560 | Nevada | 130 |
| Arkansas | 330 | New Hampshire | 70 |
| California | 4,510 | New Jersey | 710 |
| Colorado | 380 | New Mexico | 290 |
| Connecticut | 290 | New York | 2,330 |
| Delaware | 70 | North Carolina | 790 |
| District of Columbia | 130 | North Dakota | 90 |
| Florida | 1,460 | Ohio | 1,340 |
| Georgia | 940 | Oklahoma | 460 |
| Hawaii | 120 | Oregon | 330 |
| Idaho | 120 | Pennsylvania | 1,250 |
| Illinois | 1,480 | Rhode Island | 120 |
| Indiana | 520 | South Carolina | 460 |
| Iowa | 280 | South Dakota | 100 |
| Kansas | 280 | Tennessee | 630 |
| Kentucky | 590 | Texas | 2,630 |
| Louisiana | 760 | Utah | 220 |
| Maine | 150 | Vermont | 70 |
| Maryland | 420 | Virginia | 540 |
| Massachusetts | 570 | Washington | 570 |
| Michigan | 1,240 | West Virginia | 270 |
| Minnesota | 390 | Wisconsin | 490 |
| Mississippi | 840 | Wyoming | 60 |
| Missouri | 650 | Other[19] | 3,930 |

**Relative to the President's Budget, more than 35,000 of the Nation's most vulnerable children would lose access to Head Start services under sequestration in 2016.**

---

[18] Because the Republican budgets do not provide specific discretionary program levels, this analysis assumes an overall nominal percentage reduction in available non-defense discretionary funds of 1.5 percent below currently enacted 2015 levels, applied mechanically across-the-board to all discretionary programs. To prevent cuts of this magnitude in any specific program would require deeper cuts than described in other programs. Numbers displayed are rounded.

[19] Includes children served in programs in Guam, the Northern Marianas, Puerto Rico, the Virgin Islands, American Samoa, Palau, Migrant Programs, and Indian Tribes.

| State | Funding Reduction ($ million) | Equivalent to Fewer | | | State | Funding Reduction ($ million) | Equivalent to Fewer | | |
|---|---|---|---|---|---|---|---|---|---|
| | | Schools | Teachers | Students | | | Schools | Teachers | Students |
| Alabama | 17.9 | 70 | 250 | 33,700 | Montana | 4.2 | 60 | 60 | 4,800 |
| Alaska | 3.5 | 20 | 50 | 3,800 | Nebraska | 5.9 | 40 | 80 | 8,900 |
| Arizona | 27.3 | 100 | 380 | 21,800 | Nevada | 11.2 | 20 | 150 | 21,800 |
| Arkansas | 11.7 | 60 | 160 | 20,300 | New Hampshire | 3.6 | 20 | 50 | 2,100 |
| California | 147.6 | 500 | 2030 | 293,000 | New Jersey | 28.6 | 120 | 390 | 32,700 |
| Colorado | 12.3 | 50 | 170 | 15,700 | New Mexico | 10.2 | 50 | 140 | 19,900 |
| Connecticut | 9.4 | 40 | 130 | 9,000 | New York | 103.2 | 300 | 1420 | 147,400 |
| Delaware | 4.1 | 10 | 60 | 6,900 | North Carolina | 36.7 | 110 | 510 | 54,200 |
| District of Columbia | 3.9 | 20 | 50 | 5,600 | North Dakota | 3.2 | 30 | 40 | 2,800 |
| Florida | 74.5 | 160 | 1030 | 112,700 | Ohio | 44.5 | 180 | 610 | 60,200 |
| Georgia | 41.9 | 130 | 580 | 79,500 | Oklahoma | 12.8 | 100 | 180 | 32,500 |
| Hawaii | 4.2 | 20 | 60 | 10,900 | Oregon | 11.3 | 40 | 160 | 14,700 |
| Idaho | 4.5 | 30 | 60 | 9,800 | Pennsylvania | 44.1 | 140 | 610 | 48,700 |
| Illinois | 58.2 | 210 | 800 | 68,500 | Rhode Island | 4.2 | 10 | 60 | 4,400 |
| Indiana | 20.4 | 70 | 280 | 22,400 | South Carolina | 19.9 | 40 | 270 | 24,200 |
| Iowa | 7.6 | 50 | 100 | 8,200 | South Dakota | 4.1 | 30 | 60 | 3,700 |
| Kansas | 8.6 | 50 | 120 | 11,700 | Tennessee | 25.0 | 90 | 340 | 44,700 |
| Kentucky | 16.9 | 70 | 230 | 36,400 | Texas | 112.9 | 480 | 1550 | 277,700 |
| Louisiana | 23.4 | 70 | 320 | 37,300 | Utah | 7.9 | 30 | 110 | 11,500 |
| Maine | 4.2 | 30 | 60 | 2,800 | Vermont | 3.1 | 20 | 40 | 4,300 |
| Maryland | 18.4 | 30 | 250 | 15,000 | Virginia | 20.0 | 60 | 280 | 20,700 |
| Massachusetts | 19.6 | 80 | 270 | 25,500 | Washington | 18.7 | 70 | 260 | 27,200 |
| Michigan | 32.5 | 120 | 450 | 39,000 | West Virginia | 7.4 | 30 | 100 | 9,200 |
| Minnesota | 12.5 | 70 | 170 | 15,500 | Wisconsin | 18.3 | 100 | 250 | 24,600 |
| Mississippi | 14.9 | 50 | 210 | 26,900 | Wyoming | 3.1 | 20 | 40 | 2,300 |
| Missouri | 18.6 | 80 | 260 | 26,300 | Puerto Rico | 21.3 | 70 | 290 | 22,500 |

**Relative to the President's Budget, sequestration would result in a $1.2 billion reduction in Title I, approximately equivalent to funding for 4,500 schools, 17,000 teachers and aides, and 1.9 million students.[22]**

[20] Because the Republican budgets do not provide specific discretionary program levels, this analysis assumes an overall nominal percentage reduction in available non-defense discretionary funds of 1.5 percent below currently enacted 2015 levels, applied mechanically across-the-board to all discretionary programs. To prevent cuts of this magnitude in any specific program would require deeper cuts than described in other programs. Numbers displayed are rounded.

[21] This table does not include $12.2 million in cuts to other non-state allocations.

## INDIVIDUALS WITH DISABILITIES EDUCATION ACT (IDEA) STATE GRANTS, PART B [23,24]

| State | Funding Reduction ($ million) | Funding Reduction (%) | State | Funding Reduction ($ millions) | Funding Reduction (%) |
|---|---|---|---|---|---|
| Alabama | 5.1 | 2.9 | Montana | 1.2 | 3.1 |
| Alaska | 1.2 | 3.2 | Nebraska | 2.1 | 2.8 |
| Arizona | 8.8 | 4.7 | Nevada | 3.3 | 4.7 |
| Arkansas | 3.2 | 2.9 | New Hampshire | 1.3 | 2.8 |
| California | 35.3 | 2.9 | New Jersey | 10.0 | 2.8 |
| Colorado | 4.6 | 3.0 | New Mexico | 2.5 | 2.8 |
| Connecticut | 3.7 | 2.8 | New York | 21.2 | 2.8 |
| Delaware | 1.3 | 3.6 | North Carolina | 9.7 | 3.0 |
| District of Columbia | 0.8 | 4.7 | North Dakota | 1.3 | 4.7 |
| Florida | 18.3 | 2.9 | Ohio | 12.5 | 2.9 |
| Georgia | 15.3 | 4.6 | Oklahoma | 4.2 | 2.9 |
| Hawaii | 1.1 | 2.9 | Oregon | 3.7 | 2.9 |
| Idaho | 1.6 | 3.0 | Pennsylvania | 12.2 | 2.9 |
| Illinois | 14.2 | 2.8 | Rhode Island | 1.21 | 2.8 |
| Indiana | 7.2 | 2.8 | South Carolina | 5.0 | 2.8 |
| Iowa | 3.4 | 2.8 | South Dakota | 1.6 | 4.7 |
| Kansas | 3.0 | 2.9 | Tennessee | 6.8 | 2.9 |
| Kentucky | 4.4 | 2.8 | Texas | 29.2 | 3.0 |
| Louisiana | 5.5 | 2.9 | Utah | 5.1 | 4.6 |
| Maine | 1.5 | 2.8 | Vermont | 1.3 | 4.7 |
| Maryland | 5.6 | 2.8 | Virginia | 8.1 | 2.9 |
| Massachusetts | 7.9 | 2.8 | Washington | 6.4 | 2.9 |
| Michigan | 11.5 | 2.9 | West Virginia | 2.1 | 2.8 |
| Minnesota | 5.3 | 2.8 | Wisconsin | 5.9 | 2.8 |
| Mississippi | 3.5 | 2.9 | Wyoming | 1.3 | 4.7 |
| Missouri | 6.3 | 2.8 | Other[25] | 6.8 | 3.2 |

**Relative to the President's Budget, in 2016 sequestration would reduce Federal IDEA grants by $347 million, equivalent to the amount necessary to support up to 6,000 special education teachers and staff.**

[22] These figures represent the equivalent number of schools, students, and teachers that the funding cut could support; actual impact is dependent on the decisions of the districts receiving the lower allocations.

[23] Because the Republican budgets do not provide specific discretionary program levels, this analysis assumes an overall nominal percentage reduction in available non-defense discretionary funds of 1.5 percent below currently enacted 2015 levels, applied mechanically across-the-board to all discretionary programs. To prevent cuts of this magnitude in any specific program would require deeper cuts than described in other programs. Numbers displayed are rounded.

[24] This table does not include $2 million in cuts to the set-aside for technical assistance under IDEA Section 611(c).

[25] Includes reduction in IDEA funding to Puerto Rico and the Department of Interior's Bureau of Indian Education.

| State | Fewer Participants | State | Fewer Participants |
|-------|-------------------|-------|-------------------|
| Alabama | 28,900 | Montana | 16,700 |
| Alaska | 24,500 | Nebraska | 18,800 |
| Arizona | 42,500 | Nevada | 20,700 |
| Arkansas | 18,000 | New Hampshire | 9,000 |
| California | 269,800 | New Jersey | 64,600 |
| Colorado | 36,200 | New Mexico | 18,700 |
| Connecticut | 25,800 | New York | 130,600 |
| Delaware | 6,300 | North Carolina | 65,900 |
| District of Columbia | 7,100 | North Dakota | 17,000 |
| Florida | 130,500 | Ohio | 79,800 |
| Georgia | 67,500 | Oklahoma | 22,000 |
| Hawaii | 8,000 | Oregon | 27,500 |
| Idaho | 20,400 | Pennsylvania | 87,000 |
| Illinois | 94,300 | Rhode Island | 8,300 |
| Indiana | 43,400 | South Carolina | 30,600 |
| Iowa | 20,500 | South Dakota | 15,700 |
| Kansas | 18,700 | Tennessee | 42,800 |
| Kentucky | 28,800 | Texas | 163,900 |
| Louisiana | 27,500 | Utah | 21,400 |
| Maine | 12,100 | Vermont | 7,400 |
| Maryland | 40,600 | Virginia | 53,900 |
| Massachusetts | 46,200 | Washington | 46,800 |
| Michigan | 71,600 | West Virginia | 18,000 |
| Minnesota | 37,200 | Wisconsin | 40,100 |
| Mississippi | 19,100 | Wyoming | 12,200 |
| Missouri | 40,700 | Other[27] | 28,700 |

**In 2016, sequestration funding levels would mean 2.2 million fewer people would receive employment and training services, as compared to the President's Budget.**

[26] Because the Republican budgets do not provide specific discretionary program levels, this analysis assumes an overall nominal percentage reduction in available non-defense discretionary funds of 1.5 percent below currently enacted 2015 levels, applied mechanically across-the-board to all discretionary programs. To prevent cuts of this magnitude in any specific program would require deeper cuts than described in other programs. Numbers displayed are rounded.
[27] Includes Puerto Rico and the Freely Associated States.

| State | Funding Reduction ($ million) | Vouchers Lost | State | Funding Reduction ($ million) | Vouchers Lost |
|---|---|---|---|---|---|
| Alabama | 17.6 | 1,840 | Montana | 2.9 | 310 |
| Alaska | 3.5 | 240 | Nebraska | 6.2 | 740 |
| Arizona | 15.9 | 1,370 | Nevada | 12.6 | 920 |
| Arkansas | 8.8 | 1,220 | New Hampshire | 7.9 | 620 |
| California | 321.2 | 18,530 | New Jersey | 68.7 | 4,050 |
| Colorado | 22.4 | 1,890 | New Mexico | 6.8 | 710 |
| Connecticut | 34.9 | 2,190 | New York | 229.9 | 13,620 |
| Delaware | 3.9 | 300 | North Carolina | 32.9 | 3,320 |
| DC | 18.0 | 670 | North Dakota | 3.0 | 390 |
| Florida | 80.2 | 5,990 | Ohio | 52.4 | 5,660 |
| Georgia | 46.2 | 3,250 | Oklahoma | 12.1 | 1,400 |
| Hawaii | 10.5 | 580 | Oregon | 20.9 | 2,050 |
| Idaho | 3.6 | 410 | Pennsylvania | 55.8 | 4,620 |
| Illinois | 80.6 | 5,040 | Rhode Island | 8.0 | 610 |
| Indiana | 19.5 | 2,130 | South Carolina | 13.7 | 1,510 |
| Iowa | 9.1 | 1,230 | South Dakota | 2.7 | 330 |
| Kansas | 5.8 | 710 | Tennessee | 20.3 | 2,190 |
| Kentucky | 18.5 | 1,830 | Texas | 98.2 | 8,920 |
| Louisiana | 32.5 | 2,900 | Utah | 6.9 | 710 |
| Maine | 8.2 | 740 | Vermont | 4.7 | 460 |
| Maryland | 50.7 | 2,720 | Virginia | 37.5 | 2,730 |
| Massachusetts | 84.2 | 5,010 | Washington | 42.7 | 3,200 |
| Michigan | 33.2 | 3,200 | West Virginia | 6.3 | 840 |
| Minnesota | 21.3 | 1,940 | Wisconsin | 14.5 | 1,570 |
| Mississippi | 13.2 | 1,360 | Wyoming | 1.3 | 140 |
| Missouri | 22.8 | 2,360 | Other | 23.1 | 1,960 |

**At sequestration levels HUD would provide $2.1 billion less funding for Housing Choice Vouchers, resulting in 133,000 fewer families getting help relative to the President's Budget.**

[28] Because the Republican budgets do not provide specific discretionary program levels, this analysis assumes an overall nominal percentage reduction in available non-defense discretionary funds of 1.5 percent below currently enacted 2015 levels, applied mechanically across-the-board to all discretionary programs. To prevent cuts of this magnitude in any specific program would require deeper cuts than described in other programs. Estimated state funding reductions and voucher cuts are based on 2015 enacted formula allocations. Numbers displayed are rounded.

[29] This table does not include an additional $343 million in undistributed cuts.

| State | Federal Aid Highway Grants ($ million) | Transit Formula Grants ($ million) | State | Federal Aid Highway Grants ($ million) | Transit Formula Grants ($ million) |
|---|---|---|---|---|---|
| Alabama | 824.5 | 54.1 | Montana | 386.2 | 26.5 |
| Alaska | 582.5 | 68.9 | Nebraska | 289.6 | 32.3 |
| Arizona | 747.3 | 148.2 | Nevada | 338.5 | 70.1 |
| Arkansas | 550.3 | 32.3 | New Hampshire | 167.3 | 16.8 |
| California | 3,805.6 | 787.7 | New Jersey | 700.7 | 921.2 |
| Colorado | 706.7 | 144.8 | New Mexico | 361.2 | 63.3 |
| Connecticut | 476.2 | 327.9 | New York | 1,869.0 | 1,834.7 |
| Delaware | 206.9 | 19.3 | North Carolina | 969.2 | 156.1 |
| District of Columbia | 152.7 | 295.8 | North Dakota | 260.9 | 18.5 |
| Florida | 1,810.0 | 321.7 | Ohio | 1,347.4 | 286.4 |
| Georgia | 1,273.3 | 309.9 | Oklahoma | 625.3 | 28.5 |
| Hawaii | 157.2 | 54.8 | Oregon | 461.6 | 214.8 |
| Idaho | 286.2 | 21.9 | Pennsylvania | 1,555.4 | 615.1 |
| Illinois | 1,428.1 | 848.1 | Rhode Island | 222.1 | 72.6 |
| Indiana | 981.6 | 134.7 | South Carolina | 671.3 | 38.6 |
| Iowa | 505.3 | 63.6 | South Dakota | 315.5 | 20.4 |
| Kansas | 364.2 | 44.9 | Tennessee | 799.0 | 115.8 |
| Kentucky | 686.0 | 100.6 | Texas | 3,556.5 | 420.2 |
| Louisiana | 749.9 | 50.7 | Utah | 346.0 | 57.4 |
| Maine | 181.6 | 21.4 | Vermont | 210.3 | 50.2 |
| Maryland | 527.5 | 376.5 | Virginia | 974.5 | 168.1 |
| Massachusetts | 638.6 | 425.4 | Washington | 711.7 | 320.2 |
| Michigan | 1,009.8 | 210.2 | West Virginia | 421.0 | 27.3 |
| Minnesota | 654.1 | 191.7 | Wisconsin | 805.5 | 178.8 |
| Mississippi | 498.6 | 10.8 | Wyoming | 257.0 | 21.1 |
| Missouri | 928.6 | 162.6 | Other[31] | 165.8 | 126.3 |

**The Republican budgets put at risk over $50.6 billion provided to states in 2014 to support highways and mass transit systems through the Federal Aid Highways and Transit Formula Grants programs.**

[30] Because the Republican budgets do not provide specific discretionary program levels, and because Congress has not yet enacted full-year authorizations for surface transportation programs, this analysis is based on FY 2014 actual funding levels. Numbers displayed are rounded.
[31] Includes Guam, the Northern Marianas, Puerto Rico, the Virgin Islands, American Samoa, the Freely Associated States, and other undistributed funding.

## PLANNED CONSTRUCTION & MAINTENANCE AT NATIONAL PARKS DELAYED OR CANCELLED [32]

### Alabama
- Horseshoe Bend National Military Park*
- Selma to Montgomery Historic Trail*

### Alaska
- Denali National Park and Preserve*
- Glacier Bay National park and Preserve
- Katmai National Park and Preserve*
- Kenai Fjords National Park
- Klondike Gold Rush National Historical Park
- Sitka National Historic Park
- Wrangell-Saint Elias National Park and Preserve*

### Arizona
- Casa Grande Ruins National Monument
- Fort Bowie National Historic Site
- Glen Canyon National Recreation Area
- Grand Canyon National Park
- Grand Canyon-Parashant National Monument
- Petrified Forest National Park
- Wupatki National Monument
- Saguaro National Park*

### Arkansas
- Buffalo National River*
- Hot Springs National Park

### California
- Cabrillo National Monument
- Channel Islands National Park
- Death Valley National Park*
- Eugene O'Neill National Historic Site
- Fort Point National Historic Site
- Golden Gate National Recreation Area
- Lassen Volcanic National Park
- Manzanar National Historic Site
- Point Reyes National Seashore
- Redwood National Park
- San Francisco Maritime National Historical Park
- Santa Monica Mountains National Recreation Area
- Sequoia and Kings Canyon National Park
- Whiskeytown National Recreation Area
- Yosemite National Park*
- Mojave National Preserve*

### Colorado
- Bent's Old Fort National Historic Site
- Curecanti National Recreation Area*
- Dinosaur National Monument
- Florissant Fossil Beds National Monument
- Great Sand Dunes National Park and Preserve
- Mesa Verde National Park*
- Rocky Mountain National Park

### D.C
- National Capital Parks- East
- The White House
- National Mall and Memorial Parks*

### Florida
- Biscayne National Park
- Castillo De San Marcos National Monument

### Georgia
- Chattahoochee River National Recreation Area
- Kennesaw Mountain National Battlefield Park
- Appalachian National Scenic Trail
- Martin Luther King Jr. National Historic Site*

### Hawaii
- Heleakala National Park
- Hawaii Volcanoes National Park
- Kalaupapa National Historical Park
- World War II Valor in The Pacific National Monument

### Idaho
- Craters Of The Moon National Preserve
- Minidoka National Historic Site

### Iowa
- Herbert Hoover National Historic Site

### Kansas
- Fort Larned National Historic Site

### Louisiana
- Cane River Creole National Historical Park

### Maryland
- Assateague Island National Seashore
- Chesapeake and Ohio Canal National Historical Park*
- Fort McHenry National Monument and Historic Shrine
- Hampton National Historic Site

### Maine
- Acadia National Park
- Appalachian National Scenic Trail

---

[32] Asterisk represents planned major construction projects in 2016.

## Massachusetts
- Adams National Historical Park
- Boston National Historical Park
- Cape Cod National Seashore*
- Lowell National Historical Park
- Minute Man National Historical Park
- Salem Maritime National Historic Site

## Michigan
- Isle Royal National Park
- Keweenaw National Historical Park
- Sleeping Bear Dunes National Lakeshore

## Minnesota
- Voyageurs National Park

## Mississippi
- Gulf Islands National Seashore
- Vicksburg National Military Park*

## Missouri
- Ozark National Scenic Riverways

## Montana
- Bighorn Canyon National Recreation Area
- Glacier National Park
- Bighorn Canyon National Recreation Area

## Nebraska
- Scotts Bluff National Monument

## New Hampshire
- Appalachian National Scenic Trail
- Saint-Gaudens National Historic Site

## New Jersey
- Thomas Edison National Historical Park
- Appalachian National Scenic Trail

## New Mexico
- Capulin Volcano National Monument
- Chaco Culture National Historical park
- El Morro National Monument
- Pecos National Historical Park
- White Sands National Monument
- Bandelier National Monument*
- Old Santa Fe Trail Building*

## New York
- Fire Island National Seashore
- Fort Stanwix National Monument
- Home of Franklin D. Roosevelt National Historic Site

## North Carolina
- Blue Ridge Parkway
- Carl Sandburg Home National Historic Site
- Moores Creek National Battlefield
- Appalachian National Scenic Trail
- Cape Hatteras National Seashore*
- Guilford Courthouse National Military Park*

## Northern Mariana Islands
- American Memorial Park

## Oklahoma
- Chickasaw National Recreation Area

## Pennsylvania
- Allegheny Portage Railroad National Historic Site*
- Delaware Water Gap National Recreation Area
- Eisenhower National Historic Site
- Fort Necessity National Battlefield
- Johnstown Flood National Memorial
- Valley Forge National Historical Park*
- Appalachian National Scenic Trail

## Puerto Rico
- San Juan National Historic Site

## South Carolina
- Fort Sumter National Monument

## South Dakota
- Badlands National Park
- Mount Rushmore National Memorial
- Wine Cave National Park

## Tennessee
- Andrew Johnson National Historic Site
- Great Smoky Mountains National Park
- Appalachian National Scenic Trail
- Obed Wild and Scenic River*

## Texas
- Guadalupe Mountains National Park
- Lyndon B. Johnson National Historical Park

## Utah
- Bryce Canyon National Park
- Canyonlands National Park
- Capitol Reef National Park
- Cedar Breaks National Monument
- Hovenweep National Memorial
- Timpanogos Cave National Monument*

## Vermont
- Marsh-Billings-Rockefeller National Historical Park

## Virginia
- Cedar Creek and Belle Grove National Historical Park*
- Colonial National Historical Park
- Cumberland Gap National Historical Park
- Fredericksburg and Spotsylvania National Military Park*
- Maggie L. Walker National Historic Site
- Richmond National Battlefield Park
- Shenandoah National Park
- Appalachian National Scenic Trail

## Virgin Islands
- Christiansted National Historic Site

## Washington
- Fort Vancouver National Historic Site
- Mount Rainier National Park
- North Cascades National Park
- Olympic National Park
- San Juan Island National Historical Park

## West Virginia
- Harpers Ferry National Historical Park

## Wisconsin
- Apostle Islands National Lakeshore

## Wyoming
- Bighorn Canyon National Recreation Area
- Fort Laramie National Historic Site
- Yellowstone National Park
- Bighorn Canyon National Recreation Area
- Grand Teton National Park*

**At our national parks, sequestration would delay 26 of the 35 major construction projects and 208 of the 464 rehabilitation projects proposed in the President's Budget.**

## SUPPLEMENTAL NUTRITION ASSISTANCE PROGRAM [33,34]

| State | 5-Year Cut ($ million) | Current Beneficiaries[35] | State | 5-Year Cut ($ million) | Current Beneficiaries |
|---|---|---|---|---|---|
| Alabama | 2,100 | 902,000 | Montana | 300 | 125,000 |
| Alaska | 300 | 87,000 | Nebraska | 400 | 174,000 |
| Arizona | 2,300 | 1,044,000 | Nevada | 900 | 384,000 |
| Arkansas | 1,100 | 492,000 | New Hampshire | 200 | 112,000 |
| California | 11,800 | 4,350,000 | New Jersey | 2,000 | 883,000 |
| Colorado | 1,200 | 505,000 | New Mexico | 1,000 | 431,000 |
| Connecticut | 1,100 | 439,000 | New York | 8,200 | 3,123,000 |
| Delaware | 300 | 150,000 | North Carolina | 3,800 | 1,576,000 |
| District of Columbia | 400 | 143,000 | North Dakota | 100 | 54,000 |
| Florida | 8,700 | 3,526,000 | Ohio | 4,100 | 1,752,000 |
| Georgia | 4,500 | 1,816,000 | Oklahoma | 1,400 | 608,000 |
| Hawaii | 800 | 194,000 | Oregon | 1,800 | 802,000 |
| Idaho | 500 | 212,000 | Pennsylvania | 4,100 | 1,796,000 |
| Illinois | 5,100 | 2,015,000 | Rhode Island | 400 | 179,000 |
| Indiana | 2,100 | 893,000 | South Carolina | 2,000 | 835,000 |
| Iowa | 800 | 408,000 | South Dakota | 200 | 101,000 |
| Kansas | 600 | 293,000 | Tennessee | 3,100 | 1,313,000 |
| Kentucky | 1,900 | 828,000 | Texas | 8,500 | 3,853,000 |
| Louisiana | 2,000 | 877,000 | Utah | 500 | 230,000 |
| Maine | 500 | 231,000 | Vermont | 200 | 93,000 |
| Maryland | 1,800 | 788,000 | Virginia | 2,100 | 919,000 |
| Massachusetts | 2,000 | 863,000 | Washington | 2,500 | 1,096,000 |
| Michigan | 4,100 | 1,679,000 | West Virginia | 800 | 363,000 |
| Minnesota | 1,100 | 534,000 | Wisconsin | 1,800 | 842,000 |
| Mississippi | 1,400 | 657,000 | Wyoming | 100 | 36,000 |
| Missouri | 2,000 | 858,000 | Guam & Virgin Islands | 300 | 75,000 |

**The House Republican budget would convert SNAP to a block grant and cut funding by about $125 billion over the 2021-2025 period, jeopardizing nutrition assistance for the more than 46 million Americans who depend on it.**

[33] Source: Center on Budget and Policy Priorities (http://www.cbpp.org/cms/index.cfm?fa=view&id=5287).
[34] This table does not include an additional $14 billion reduction in funding for the federal share of administrative costs, nutrition assistance in Puerto Rico and American Samoa, funding for food banks, and for the Food Distribution Program on Indian Reservations (FDPIR).
[35] Reflects average monthly participation for FY 2014. Numbers displayed are rounded.

| State | Current Recipients[36] | State | Current Recipients |
|---|---|---|---|
| Alabama | 153,000 | Montana | 22,000 |
| Alaska | 11,000 | Nebraska | 39,000 |
| Arizona | 403,000 | Nevada | 35,000 |
| Arkansas | 83,000 | New Hampshire | 23,000 |
| California | 1,027,000 | New Jersey | 173,000 |
| Colorado | 133,000 | New Mexico | 59,000 |
| Connecticut | 71,000 | New York | 494,000 |
| Delaware | 16,000 | North Carolina | 215,000 |
| District of Columbia | 38,000 | North Dakota | 13,000 |
| Florida | 572,000 | Ohio | 260,000 |
| Georgia | 275,000 | Oklahoma | 91,000 |
| Hawaii | 22,000 | Oregon | 114,000 |
| Idaho | 54,000 | Pennsylvania | 262,000 |
| Illinois | 352,000 | Rhode Island | 31,000 |
| Indiana | 182,000 | South Carolina | 115,000 |
| Iowa | 112,000 | South Dakota | 25,000 |
| Kansas | 72,000 | Tennessee | 164,000 |
| Kentucky | 118,000 | Texas | 605,000 |
| Louisiana | 110,000 | Utah | 115,000 |
| Maine | 27,000 | Vermont | 12,000 |
| Maryland | 109,000 | Virginia | 188,000 |
| Massachusetts | 131,000 | Washington | 130,000 |
| Michigan | 269,000 | West Virginia | 63,000 |
| Minnesota | 146,000 | Wisconsin | 117,000 |
| Mississippi | 99,000 | Wyoming | 12,000 |
| Missouri | 165,000 | Other[37] | 249,000 |

The House Republican budget calls for freezing Pell Grants and eliminates more than $90 billion in Pell funding over the next decade, eroding benefits and harming the more than 8 million students who now use Pell Grants to help pay for college.

[36] Numbers displayed are rounded.
[37] Includes Guam, the Northern Marianas, Puerto Rico, the Virgin Islands, American Samoa, Palau, and Micronesia.

| State | Plans Selected | State | Plans Selected |
|---|---|---|---|
| Alabama | 172,000 | Montana | 54,000 |
| Alaska | 21,000 | Nebraska | 74,000 |
| Arizona | 206,000 | Nevada | 74,000 |
| Arkansas | 66,000 | New Hampshire | 53,000 |
| California | 1,412,000 | New Jersey | 254,000 |
| Colorado | 140,000 | New Mexico | 52,000 |
| Connecticut | 110,000 | New York | 409,000 |
| Delaware | 25,000 | North Carolina | 560,000 |
| District of Columbia | 18,000 | North Dakota | 18,000 |
| Florida | 1,596,000 | Ohio | 234,000 |
| Georgia | 541,000 | Oklahoma | 126,000 |
| Hawaii | 13,000 | Oregon | 112,000 |
| Idaho | 97,000 | Pennsylvania | 473,000 |
| Illinois | 349,000 | Rhode Island | 31,000 |
| Indiana | 219,000 | South Carolina | 210,000 |
| Iowa | 45,000 | South Dakota | 21,000 |
| Kansas | 96,000 | Tennessee | 231,000 |
| Kentucky | 106,000 | Texas | 1,205,000 |
| Louisiana | 186,000 | Utah | 141,000 |
| Maine | 75,000 | Vermont | 32,000 |
| Maryland | 120,000 | Virginia | 385,000 |
| Massachusetts | 141,000 | Washington | 161,000 |
| Michigan | 341,000 | West Virginia | 33,000 |
| Minnesota | 60,000 | Wisconsin | 207,000 |
| Mississippi | 105,000 | Wyoming | 21,000 |
| Missouri | 253,000 | | |

**The Republican budgets would take away Marketplace coverage from 11.7 million Americans who have newly signed up or been re-enrolled in coverage for 2015 under the Affordable Care Act.**

[38] Source: Health Insurance Marketplaces 2015 Open Enrollment Period: March Enrollment Report. (http://www.aspe.hhs.gov/health/reports/2015/MarketPlaceEnrollment/Mar2015/ib_2015mar_enrollment.pdf.)

[39] These data generally represent the number of individuals who have selected, or been automatically reenrolled into a 2015 plan through the Marketplaces, with or without payment of premium ("preeffectuated enrollment"). Enrollment is considered effectuated when the first premium payment is made, and this figure includes plan selections for which enrollment has not yet been effectuated. Data on effectuated enrollment are not yet available. Reenrollment data in this report may include some individuals who were reenrolled in coverage through the Marketplaces as of 2-15-15 (including special enrollment period activity through 2-22-15), but who may ultimately decide not to retain Marketplace coverage for the remainder of 2015 (for example, because they have obtained coverage through another source). Numbers displayed are rounded.

| State | Current Beneficiaries | Average Discount ($) | State | Current Beneficiaries | Average Discount ($) |
|---|---|---|---|---|---|
| Alabama | 89,300 | 930 | Montana | 13,100 | 800 |
| Alaska | 3,200 | 960 | Nebraska | 29,700 | 800 |
| Arizona | 95,200 | 870 | Nevada | 33,000 | 870 |
| Arkansas | 40,500 | 780 | New Hampshire | 18,900 | 900 |
| California | 417,500 | 940 | New Jersey | 214,300 | 1,140 |
| Colorado | 58,800 | 880 | New Mexico | 24,100 | 890 |
| Connecticut | 60,600 | 1,070 | New York | 353,100 | 1,080 |
| Delaware | 23,900 | 1,090 | North Carolina | 174,500 | 880 |
| District of Columbia | 3,200 | 960 | North Dakota | 11,300 | 850 |
| Florida | 346,100 | 880 | Ohio | 239,700 | 980 |
| Georgia | 141,600 | 930 | Oklahoma | 65,200 | 930 |
| Hawaii | 24,100 | 1,090 | Oregon | 52,600 | 810 |
| Idaho | 18,900 | 780 | Pennsylvania | 297,100 | 950 |
| Illinois | 194,300 | 930 | Rhode Island | 16,300 | 820 |
| Indiana | 126,500 | 930 | South Carolina | 98,900 | 970 |
| Iowa | 54,300 | 850 | South Dakota | 13,100 | 800 |
| Kansas | 46,800 | 830 | Tennessee | 112,100 | 840 |
| Kentucky | 92,000 | 980 | Texas | 345,500 | 950 |
| Louisiana | 73,300 | 850 | Utah | 27,200 | 840 |
| Maine | 17,300 | 870 | Vermont | 9,700 | 950 |
| Maryland | 79,900 | 1,030 | Virginia | 112,000 | 910 |
| Massachusetts | 79,800 | 920 | Washington | 72,400 | 860 |
| Michigan | 205,200 | 1,050 | West Virginia | 45,500 | 1,040 |
| Minnesota | 69,200 | 860 | Wisconsin | 89,400 | 910 |
| Mississippi | 41,400 | 750 | Wyoming | 7,900 | 850 |
| Missouri | 109,000 | 870 | Other[41] | 13,100 | 3,500 |

**The Republican budgets would increase prescription drug costs for more than 5 million seniors and people with disabilities.**

---

[40] Data for the year 2014, as of December 2014. Numbers displayed are rounded.
[41] Includes Guam, the Northern Marianas, Puerto Rico, and the Virgin Islands.

| State | Block Grant Cut 2016-2025[42] ($ billion) | State | Block Grant Cut 2016-2025 ($ billion) |
|---|---|---|---|
| Alabama | 11.6 | Montana | 2.4 |
| Alaska | 2.8 | Nebraska | 3.3 |
| Arizona | 20.9 | Nevada | 5.3 |
| Arkansas | 11.8 | New Hampshire | 2.3 |
| California | 119.2 | New Jersey | 23.2 |
| Colorado | 11.0 | New Mexico | 10.1 |
| Connecticut | 12.7 | New York | 88.1 |
| Delaware | 3.4 | North Carolina | 26.0 |
| District of Columbia | 5.6 | North Dakota | 0.7 |
| Florida | 38.7 | Ohio | 42.0 |
| Georgia | 20.6 | Oklahoma | 10.0 |
| Hawaii | 3.7 | Oregon | 16.2 |
| Idaho | 3.8 | Pennsylvania | 41.2 |
| Illinois | 29.8 | Rhode Island | 4.6 |
| Indiana | 20.0 | South Carolina | 12.3 |
| Iowa | 8.0 | South Dakota | 1.5 |
| Kansas | 5.3 | Tennessee | 19.6 |
| Kentucky | 18.9 | Texas | 60.9 |
| Louisiana | 14.2 | Utah | 4.9 |
| Maine | 4.9 | Vermont | 2.9 |
| Maryland | 17.1 | Virginia | 12.8 |
| Massachusetts | 24.0 | Washington | 13.9 |
| Michigan | 30.1 | West Virginia | 7.9 |
| Minnesota | 17.7 | Wisconsin | 14.5 |
| Mississippi | 11.4 | Wyoming | 1.0 |
| Missouri | 18.0 | | |

**In next decade, the Medicaid block grant proposal in the House Republican budget would cut Medicaid and Children's Health Insurance Program funding to states by more than $900 billion, resulting in a more than 20 percent cut to projected program spending.**

[42] Assumed reductions based on the House block grant proposal and the proportion of each state's spending in FY 2014. In addition to these cuts, more than $800 billion would be cut from Medicaid nation-wide due to the repeal of the ACA Medicaid expansion. Numbers displayed are rounded.

| State | Total Benefits, 2015 ($ million) | Families Losing Benefits | State | Total Benefits, 2015 ($ million) | Families Losing Benefits |
|---|---|---|---|---|---|
| Alabama | 274 | 304,000 | Montana | 40 | 47,000 |
| Alaska | 24 | 27,000 | Nebraska | 73 | 81,000 |
| Arizona | 345 | 359,000 | Nevada | 136 | 146,000 |
| Arkansas | 161 | 179,000 | New Hampshire | 33 | 40,000 |
| California | 1,832 | 1,966,000 | New Jersey | 296 | 333,000 |
| Colorado | 200 | 223,000 | New Mexico | 118 | 126,000 |
| Connecticut | 98 | 113,000 | New York | 802 | 893,000 |
| Delaware | 35 | 39,000 | North Carolina | 498 | 552,000 |
| District of Columbia | 23 | 24,000 | North Dakota | 20 | 24,000 |
| Florida | 965 | 1,080,000 | Ohio | 490 | 546,000 |
| Georgia | 601 | 642,000 | Oklahoma | 193 | 212,000 |
| Hawaii | 50 | 57,000 | Oregon | 156 | 173,000 |
| Idaho | 80 | 88,000 | Pennsylvania | 423 | 486,000 |
| Illinois | 577 | 629,000 | Rhode Island | 37 | 42,000 |
| Indiana | 300 | 327,000 | South Carolina | 253 | 279,000 |
| Iowa | 105 | 120,000 | South Dakota | 31 | 36,000 |
| Kansas | 121 | 134,000 | Tennessee | 341 | 383,000 |
| Kentucky | 205 | 234,000 | Texas | 1,499 | 1,588,000 |
| Louisiana | 257 | 279,000 | Utah | 140 | 147,000 |
| Maine | 43 | 53,000 | Vermont | 19 | 23,000 |
| Maryland | 192 | 212,000 | Virginia | 288 | 329,000 |
| Massachusetts | 166 | 195,000 | Washington | 240 | 275,000 |
| Michigan | 429 | 472,000 | West Virginia | 76 | 91,000 |
| Minnesota | 169 | 191,000 | Wisconsin | 202 | 225,000 |
| Mississippi | 202 | 217,000 | Wyoming | 20 | 22,000 |
| Missouri | 265 | 296,000 | Other | 62 | 78,000 |

**Republicans would allow important Earned Income Tax Credit and Child Tax Credit improvements to expire after 2017, raising taxes an average of $900 for 16 million working families with children.**

[43] Source: US Department of Treasury, Office of Tax Analysis. Figures are for 2015, but figures for 2018, when improvements would expire under the Republican budgets, would be similar. Numbers displayed are rounded.